Controversies in Sociology
edited by
Professor T. B. Bottomore and Dr M. J. Mulkay

5

Social
Evolution
and
Sociological
Categories

Controversies in Sociology

Social Evolution and Sociological Categories

by
PAUL Q. HIRST

Lecturer in Sociology
Birkbeck College

Holmes & Meier Publishers
New York

First published in the United States of America 1976 by
Holmes & Meier Publishers, Inc.
101 Fifth Avenue
New York, N.Y. 10003

Library of Congress Cataloging in Publication Data
Hirst, P   Q
  Social evolution and sociological categories.

  (Controversies in sociology; 5)
  Bibliography: p.
  Includes index.
  1. Social sciences—Methodology. 2. Social evolution. 3. Social
sciences—Classification. I. Title.
H61.H54   300'.1'8   76–5413

ISBN 0-8419-0257-7

Printed in Great Britain

Acknowledgements

I would like to thank Tom Bottomore, Ben Cosin, Barry Hindess and Tom Young for their valuable criticisms and suggestions, and Mike Donnelly for his invaluable help in preparing the manuscript.

Contents

1

Introduction

This book is concerned with the relationship between classifications of and theoretical explanations of social relations. The general thesis presented here is that forms of classification are not and cannot be independent of forms of theoretical explanation. The reason for this dependence is that the very objects to be classified are constituted by definite social theories and these theories also provide the conceptual means of classification. The objects classified are not given independently of theory – categories of classification such as traditional society/industrial society or religion/magic are products of specific forms of theory.

This dependence on theory is no special attribute of classifications of social relations. All supposedly scientific forms of classification, whether of animals, languages or chemical elements, are a product of theories which constitute the objects specified and distribute them in a definite theoretical space. Classification is the recognition and mapping of this distribution. Where bodies of knowledge exhibit clear sequences of succession and discontinuity in theory then the associated classifications exhibit similar sequences, often with some lag or displacement. Classification can be discussed in the form of a *history*, of successive forms related to theories. Zoology, for example, reveals the complex and overlapping succession of the Linnean, Cuvian and evolutionary classifications of species.

Such a history is impossible in the social sciences. Such definite sequences do not exist; the major forms of theory and of classification are co-present. For example, Aristotle's, Montesquieu's and Weber's classifications of political forms continue to exist. Any attempt to produce an exhaustive survey of forms of classification of social objects would, therefore, amount to an inventory of a large number of social theories. When the editors of this series asked the author to write a text on typifications of societies and social classifications this fact became apparent. No general survey of classifications is possible which does not rapidly become an examination of the state of theory in the social sciences. In such a general examination the question of classification would take a secondary place, and the scope of such an enterprise is beyond the compass of the present work.

The approach adopted in this text, therefore, has been to confine consideration to certain specific social theories and the forms of classification engendered by them. Our general thesis is thus presented through and illustrated by specific cases. The two cases considered here have a significance which goes beyond the theme of classsification. It will be seen that an important object of this work is to differentiate the theories considered from Marxism, and in the case of Weber to challenge the status of the theory as an alternative to Marxism. The reasons why these particular theories have been chosen are given below.

In the latter half of the nineteenth century and at the beginning of the twentieth century social evolutionary theories provided the dominant classification and explanation of social institutions and types of society. Social evolutionary theories then suffered a severe decline in their fortunes. This eclipse had two main sources, the criticism of relativist and structural functionalist ethnography, and the anti-historicist critique of the philosophy of history and conjectural history. Social evolutionary theories suffered in particular from having elements in common with the vulgar conception of Marxism as a mechanistic and unilinear theory of historical progress. Recently, social evolutionism has enjoyed something of a comeback. Evolutionism has profited from the renaissance of Marxist theory; it has done so both in terms of the general reawakening of interest in systematic historical explanations and in terms of non-Marxists seeking to promote more 'respectable' theories of social change. Our discussion attempts to challenge this confusion of Marxism with social evolutionism by problematising the very category of 'evolutionism' itself. Marxism is reducible to none of the three forms of evolutionary theory outlined in the next chapter. The most important confusion of Marxism and evolutionary theory concerns the work of L. H. Morgan; here it is orthodox Marxism which has created the confusion by insisting on the identity of Morgan's form of evolutionism and historical materialism. Engels' *Origin of the Family* inserts Morgan's 'ethnical periods' into a discourse concerned with problems and using concepts very different from those of *Ancient Society*. Morgan's work is thus both borrowed and transformed by Engels. This has had complex theoretical effects. Engels' theory is dominant; Morgan's conception of the social totality is displaced and the succession of 'ethnical periods' is turned into a history determined by the economic. However, the *content* of Morgan's generalisations is adopted, rationalised and justified by Engels' Marxism. Engels borrows not Morgan's theory of society and history, but its *products*, historical generalisations. Orthodox Marxism has failed to recognise these borrowings for what they are; because it has been committed to the fundamental theoretical identity of Morgan's method and historical materialism it has been saddled with the defence of Morgan's generalisations about the evolution of kinship forms and so on. Terray represents the most sophisticated form of the attempt to justify the connection between Morgan and historical materialism; we will criticise the foundations of this justification. Marxism need not be committed to Morgan's historical generalisations.

Weber's ideal-typical method has the consequence that, for him, the theoretical foundations of the social sciences must take the form of typologies and classifications, the more or less systematic grouping of particular ideal types. Weber's types of legitimate domination and sociological categories of economic action form the substance of our second case. The nature of our approach to these questions is outlined at the beginning of Chapter 3; here we will confine ourselves to explaining why we concentrate on these particular types. Weber's conceptions of historical development, of the nature of politics and of forms of economic action form the key points of conflict with Marxism. Weber's implicit philosophy of history has been subjected to rigorous critical examination by such authors as Kolko (1959) and Mommsen (1965). Particular products of this conception of historical development such as *The Protestant Ethic and the Spirit of Capitalism* have been the subject of intensive debate. Max Weber's political thought about Germany and his personal political ideology have generated a considerable literature. Little attention has been given, however, to the logical foundations of his political and economic categories. These categories, developed in *Economy and Society*, form the core of the sociological attempt to provide alternative conceptions of politics and economics to those of Marx. Many sociologists, furthermore, consider Weber's categories as pure typifications; a relatively neutral organising framework to be preferred to the ideologically charged concepts of Marxism. We will attempt to show that these types rest upon a definite theory and that they involve a definite conception of politics and economics, a conception most certainly not free of ideology.

2

Three Forms of Evolutionary Theory

'Social evolutionism' has been largely constituted by its critics. It is the subsequent literature of criticism and commentary that has created the unitary entity 'social evolutionism' from such diverse thinkers as Comte, Morgan and Spencer. In this chapter our object will be to differentiate between the 'evolutionist' thinkers, to problematise the notion of a unitary evolutionism, to show that grouped under this apparent unity are very different theoretical enterprises indeed. This chapter takes the form of a series of differentiations – it attempts to show:

1   That there is a real difference between Darwin's and Wallace's theory of the transformation of species by natural selection and all other evolutionary theories, *biological and social*, which depend upon teleology;
2   That there is a real difference between teleological theories of human history as an evolution towards an end (Comte, Spencer) and attempts to construct a systematic and archaeological *reconstruction* of human history (Morgan).

The sequence of differentiations in this chapter is as follows:

(i) Darwin/idealistic and teleological theories of evolution *in biology*;
(ii) Darwin/Spencer;
(iii) Spencer/Morgan.

Darwin's theory, Spencer's theory and Morgan's theory will be outlined in succession.

The purpose of these differentiations is twofold. It is, firstly, to demonstrate the existence of theoretical difference itself, to indicate the three quite distinct forms of conceptualisation and explanation confused by the (untheorised) category of 'evolutionism'. Secondly, it is to indicate that the forms of classification and designation of societies, customs and living organisms established by these forms of theory are quite different and that this difference derives from the distinct nature of the forms of explanation involved. There is no such thing as a general 'evolutionary perspective' nor are there common principles of evolutionary classification.

There is more at stake in these differentiations than the scholar's due respect for intellectual complexity. The theoretical differences presented here enable us to understand better the varying fortunes of evolutionary theories in the biological and the social sciences. There is no simple differentiation of evolutionary theories into biological theories and sociological theories. Two of the forms of evolutionary theory discussed here are common to the biological and the social sciences. The theory of natural selection is, however, specific to the biological sciences. It is not because it concerns living organisms that the theory of natural selection is considered a scientific theory (other biological evolutionary theories exist), but because of its mode of explanation and the proofs which are advanced to support it. It is by means of the concepts of the theory of natural selection that we know it cannot be applied to explain the development of societies. Societies are not species; social relations cannot be explained by the physical attributes of human subjects. There is in social relations no rigorous analogue of the variation of characteristics. Social evolutionary theories have been quite different enterprises from the theory of natural selection; they have been philosophies of history or systems of historical generalisations. A scientific explanation of social development would have a different theoretical content from the theory of natural selection. Indeed, what the author would consider to be such an explanation, Marxism, bears little or no resemblance to the theory of natural selection (the relation between Marx, Morgan and Darwin is discussed later in this chapter).

1   THE NOTION OF EVOLUTION

'Evolution' is not a simple and coherent term – 'evolution' designates the most varied processes and explanations of them, varying from Lucretius to Erasmus Darwin and Charles Darwin to Benjamin Kidd. No simple reduction such as 'change through uniform causes producing successive and distinct forms' can register anything about the distinct theoretical systems in question apart from their common opposition to viewing phenomena as the effect of miracles, catastrophes, special acts of Divine Will. Any definition of the term 'evolution' will entail a definite concept of evolution, a specific theoretical system, and a specific evolutionary process constituted by that theory.

Let us begin with a definition which attempts to state the general properties of evolution in both the natural and the cultural sciences, Marshall Sahlins' outline of a concept of evolution in *Evolution and Culture*. Sahlins' conceives evolution as a single process with two aspects, Specific Evolution and General Evolution. This distinction is clear and rigorous, it attempts to reconcile two apparently distinct conceptions of evolution:

> Most definitions of evolution – whether cultural, biological, or both, is not yet relevant – are of one of two kinds. The most common calls attention to *forms* . . . and the changes . . . that occur in them. Forms and the succession of forms are the foci of concern. 'Evolution is descent with modification' or 'evolution is the succession of cultural stages' are statements in this succession-of-forms view. The second, more rarely voiced perspective conceives evolution as a grand *movement* in a certain direction and when changes in form follow that direction they are evolutionary. This perspective embraces the totality of forms, the whole of life or culture, or perhaps both and more, defining evolution by stating the direction of change of the totality. 'Evolution is movement from homogeneity to heterogeneity' is an example of the grand-movement view. [Sahlins and Service (1960) p. 6]

Sahlins conceives these two distinct positions as aspects of the evolutionary process. Evolution 'moves simultaneously in two directions':

(i) It creates *variation* through the adaptation of forms to conditions, new forms adapt and differentiate from the old;
(ii) This process of differentiation gives rise to *progress*, new forms may be higher forms than the older ones (according to definite criteria), and the general tendency of the evolutionary process is for higher forms to succeed lower ones. The process of variation

and differentiation is called Specific Evolution – it leads to successive related forms and change is to be explained in terms of adaptation. The evolution process as a whole – the tendency of which is progress – is called General Evolution. The conception of General Evolution entails a systematic classification by means of which forms are measured according to definite criteria of 'higher' and 'lower' and it entails an explanation of the overall tendency of the evolutionary process towards 'progress'.

Sahlins' attempt to unify the two forms rests on his own evolutionary meta-theory (that evolution is progress in the direction of increasing thermodynamic efficiency, and of differentiation of structure). It does, however, designate a key form of evolutionary theory common in both the natural and the social sciences. Sahlins' distinction stresses that for an evolutionary theory to designate 'higher' and 'lower' forms it must have a classification of forms, a conception of evolution as a process in a definite direction, and an explanation of why that process moves in that direction. Such theories entail a teleology (a process with a definite direction, a necessary end) and some overall 'cause' for that teleology. This is evolutionary theory based on a philosophical or pseudo-scientific system.

In speaking of a succession-of-forms approach Sahlins confuses two quite different theoretical enterprises:

(i) Historical generalisations which attempt to reconstruct the succession of forms, to order and describe specific chains of development;

(ii) Darwin's and Wallace's theory of natural selection which is neither an evolutionary system nor a history, but a general and abstract theory of the mechanism by which animal species are transformed – this theory is valid whatever the concrete successions of forms involved and specifies no necessary direction of the process of variation and transformation.

This distinction enables us to designate three forms of theory which have been called 'evolutionary':

(i) Theories, in both the natural and the social sciences, which base a tendency towards the progressive development of forms on some 'principle' or 'cause' – such theories are teleological and require the intervention of some explanatory meta-theory to account for the teleology. Such meta-theories are either philosophies (which derive 'progress' from man's attributes or from the human mind) or *Naturphilosophen* (theories of the cosmos, which explain progress in terms of some basic and universal natural principle). Examples of such theories are, in cultural evolution, Spencer and, in biological evolution, pre-Darwinians like Lamarck.

(ii) Histories of successions of forms, which reconstruct the genealogy of the current forms and describe the relations of succession. Examples of such histories are, in cultural evolution, L. H. Morgan, and in biological evolution, aspects of the work of Ernst Haeckel.

(iii) Darwin's theory is quite different from the other two types and, far from being historical or archaelogical, is not simply a reconstruction of the past but an abstract general theory applicable to all times and conditions. All times and conditions in which there are living organisms dependent on a changing environment for their sustenance and subject to laws of inheritance which involve the variation of characteristics. This theory is as abstract and universal in its explanatory scope as the Newtonian laws of motion. It is a theory which explains the formation of species in living organisms and is not merely a description of the succession of forms on this earth.

2 THE RELATION BETWEEN SOCIAL AND BIOLOGICAL EVOLUTIONISM

Until recently it was widely believed that social evolutionism owed its origin to *The Origin of Species*. Social Darwinism was an application of Darwin's theory to the study of society. This account has been shown to be erroneous. J. W. Burrow in *Evolution and Society* has demonstrated the prior origin, free of any Darwinian influence, of Spencer's conception of social evolutionism. Burrow says: 'It is only the relative dearth, in the first half of the nineteenth century, of social theories of an evolutionary kind that makes such a view plausible at all. To explain this hiatus we have to look at English intellectual life . . . in the early nineteenth century.' [Burrow (1966) p. 21] Social evolutionism developed from the problematisation of the Utilitarian tradition of Bentham and James Mill. Spencer found in Malthus' *Essay on the Principle of Population* the mechanism of his 'progress', the stimulation of population growth. His essay on population was published in 1852 – in it he developed a conception of the 'survival of the fittest'. Darwin tells us that he came to the idea of natural selection and the survival of the fittest through a reading of Malthus.

Do we not see here a new correspondence between Darwinism and social evolutionism, one in which they meet on the same level, in which Darwin is not privileged, in which they share the same ancestor, T. R. Malthus?

Such are the conjectures to which one is driven if too much dependence is placed on the methods of the history of ideas in attempting to settle theoretical questions. Darwin's own conception of his relation of Malthus is not a privileged one. Darwin's account of the role of his reading of Malthus in the genesis of his version of the theory of natural selection does not mean that natural selection is merely Malthusianism applied to the problem of the origin of species. Logically and substantively natural selection is a different theory from Malthus' principle of population. Darwin's mechanism of natural selection is not reducible to the competition of animals one with another for limited resources, a competition enforced by the tendency of population to outstrip resources. The theory of natural selection reveals the following crucial differences from this 'evolutionary Malthusianism':

(i) The role of the variation of characteristics through the opera-
    tion of the laws of inheritance – the animals that survive are
    not just the biggest, fiercest, fastest, etc., members of a species
    with given characteristics, they are biologically *variant* forms.
    Natural selection is not a competition among equivalent
    animals in which the better specimens of a given type survive.
(ii) In Darwin specific features of the environment exert 'selection
    pressures', pressures which act selectively to favour variants
    with certain characteristics. The 'fittest' is not a given, it is
    defined relative to a definite environment and selection pressure
    may act in favour of smaller and less complex variants of a
    species.

In Malthus' theory there is no process of *selection*. Malthus' thesis is simply that there are necessary mechanisms which re-store the balance between population and resources. Population pressure is not selection pressure. Its effects are largely indiscriminate; the decimation of a population through famine, fratricidal strife and pestilence. It might be argued, extending Malthus, that the most hardy specimens will tend to survive these vicissitudes. However, the 'survival of the fittest' in this case does not produce *speciation* but restores the species to equilibrium with its environment by having eliminated the weakest (and, probably, many of the strongest) members. The principle of population is deeply conservative, if accepted it explains balance and not change in living nature. Malthus' theory lacks any concept of systematic *variation* in species characteristics, hence it can have no concept of *selection pressure* (that environmental changes selectively favour certain variants).

(iii) In Darwin's theory ecological factors may systematically limit the population of a species and allow the species ample food (it inhabits a specialised ecological niche in which no other species competes for its food). Such a species suffers from no law of population increase but does suffer from other environmental selection pressures. Here Malthusianism can explain nothing whereas natural selection can, since selection pressure is not confined to population or food supply.

Whatever reading of Malthus Darwin produced, his theory of natural selection is not reducible to Malthusianism. The theory which Darwin produced at about the same time as Spencer is nothing like Spencer's, as we shall see.

3 THE THEORY OF NATURAL SELECTION

The theory of natural selection depends upon the correspondence of two distinct processes:

(i) That the reproduction of a species systematically produces variant forms with certain accentuated characteristics;

(ii) That all species live in an environment formed by the topography and the climate of a location and the other species of animals and plants that inhabit it. Such environments are subject to change and such changes systematically favour certain animals with certain variant characteristics which will tend to survive the pressures of environmental change. Variation is both created *and* transmitted by inheritance. In this theory it is the biological phenomenon of variation which produces the distinct forms on which the selection pressures of environmental change act. The 'fittest' is defined by selection pressure relative to a range of variants. The formation of a distinct line of inter-breeding variant forms depends upon further conditions and is not given in the fact of variation. Indeed, Darwin's conception of the laws of inheritance made speciation problematic. 'Blending inheritance' would tend to 'swamp' variant individuals; *see* Vorzimmer (1972).

Darwin's theory combines a theory of the effects of inheritance with an ecological theory of the source of selection pressure. To explain the formation of a distinct group of variants it is necessary to study both the forms of the species involved and the environment (which includes animal behaviour) in great detail.

A number of points need to be made to bring out the characteristics of this theory.

(i) For Darwin a *species* is not a fixed *type* (a given ensemble of characteristics which necessarily and inevitably go together – as it was for Cuvier and the classificatory morphologists) but a *population* interbreeding and with certain common but diverging characteristics: 'From these remarks it will be seen that I look at the term species, as one given for the sake of convenience to a set of individuals closely resembling each other, and that it does not essentially differ from the term variety, which is given to less distinct and more fluctuating forms.' [Darwin *The Origin of Species* p. 108] In the earlier morphologies the animal is fixed inside the armour of the attributes of its species considered as given and essential 'characteristics'. For Darwin a *species* is whatever it is, given its genetic endowment and the action of conditions, it is a group of animals interbreeding and subject to change. Hence the possibility of the development of the varied forms of life from a few simple forms.

Darwin's concept of species is radically different from the conceptions prevailing when the *Origin* was written. Darwin did not merely introduce the notion of evolutionary change into a hitherto static morphology, he shattered that morphology and the concept of species based on it. Hitherto, morphology was classificatory and based on comparative anatomy. Comparative anatomy was elaborated and systematised long before the appearance of the *Origin*, in the early 1800s by Cuvier (*see* Coleman, 1964). The designation of species and the definition of their characteristics was pre-

Darwinian in origin; its foundations were laid by Linnaeus in the eighteenth century. The system of defining species was *classificatory*, the species forming a differential series or plan. Such a classifactory system was possible because nature was considered as an accomplished entity each of whose elements was united one with another into the whole. Such conceptions of nature as a unity and of all things linked in a great chain of being depended on the notion of nature as God's creation or upon a secular substitute for God, Nature (*see* Glass *et al.*, 1959).

In these classificatory systems nature is a finite order, the species are differentiated one from another by criteria which assign each a definite class or place relative to others. The species are considered as fixed types, each having a definite and given structure. The position of the species relative to one another was fixed, each having a place assigned by its structural characteristics. It should not be thought that all the elements of the series were equivalent. The species form a series in that they are all related as elements of a definite branch of nature, but it is a differential series with a hierarchy. This hierarchy related to structural complexity or to closeness to man. The pre-evolutionary classifications therefore embody hierarchy and purpose. It is a static hierarchy of being and a purpose relative to a fixed natural order.

The acceptance of the theory of natural selection has necessarily forced a change in the basis of classification of species. Species are now generally classified genealogically, in terms of relations of descent. Evolutionary theory settled a significant problem of the earlier classifications, the subject of much debate – whether classifications were conventional and imposed on nature or corresponded to differences in nature itself.

The new system of classification did not appear all at once with the publication of the *Origin*, indeed, systematic classification by descent was only possible on the basis of the knowledges produced by using the theory. The initial effect of the acceptance of natural selection was to set the existing systematic morphology in motion. The divisions of the plan of nature became the stages of an evolutionary sequence – this is well illustrated in Rádl's discussion of the work of Haeckel in *The History of Biological Theories*. These speculative historical realignments of classifications often paraded as real accounts of development.

Such confusions were inevitable. To show the successive transformation of forms in the palaeontological record, successive chains of descent with transformation revealed in the fossil structure of animals was a vital means of winning acceptance for the Darwinian theory. Palaeontology was dominated and organised by the pre-existing systematic morphology and there was as yet no evolutionary morphology. In a vital area the theory of natural selection was forced to proceed by alien means. The classical concept of species was perpetuated of necessity by a theory which negated it.

(ii) 'I believe . . . in no law of necessary development.' [Darwin *Origin* p. 348] Darwin's theory is in Sahlins' terms, and as Sahlins realises, limited to Specific Evolution. There is no place in the logic of the theory of natural selection for a conception of evolution as progress. The theory is marked by the absence of criteria by means of which species may be ranked relative to one another as 'higher' and 'lower' forms. Natural selection defines and places forms by definite relations of descent and transformation and not by the arbitrary principles of the hierarchy of species. Complexity is measured relative to *ancestors* and not to other unrelated species. Species are not better or 'fitter' than others in some scale of relative competence. 'Fitness' is the relation of the members of a species to a given environment, a more or less satisfactory adaptation to its conditions.

To measure species relative to some standard of hierarchy or to conceive evolution as progress involves either arbitrariness or teleology. If the criteria of ranking are independent of the evolutionary process and no necessary tendency is ascribed to it then the criteria are purely evaluative and, therefore, arbitrary. A conception of evolution as progress must explain why it is that higher forms succeed lower ones – it must conceive evolution as a process impelled by necessary causes to a definite end. Evolution as progress is, paradoxically, linked with the conception of nature as finite or completed being. The conception of a hierarchy of species depends on the notion of nature embodying a finite *plan*. How otherwise can higher and lower forms be ranked and this rank order be made the order of evolutionary progress? Such theories must start from the assumption that evolution is virtually complete, man and his successors representing the apex of development, or, that evolution will proceed in the direction it has taken in the past towards some hypothesised future state (e.g. perfection). If evolution is not yet complete, its direction uncertain, and, possibly, major types of species are not yet given, then simplicity and complexity can only be relative to a *sample*. The nature of this sample of possible species, its completeness and value as a measure of hierarchy, is unknown and incalculable. It is only by assuming the finality of a *series* or *plan* that higher and lower forms can be measured without arbitrariness. Measurement of species relative to one another is made certain by the fact that the number and nature of these species is finite and given.

The notion of nature as completed being limits the function of evolutionary change to the realisation of that completeness, to the becoming of the finitude of being. Conceptions of evolution as progress generally adopted the classificatory systems of pre-evolutionary comparative anatomy as their basis of hierarchy. Comparative anatomy's serial and static tables are set in motion, evolution is the sequential fulfilment of a plan. The cause and necessity of this motion can only be explained by a *Naturphilosophie* which conceives the cosmos as a finite entity in which purpose is possible and in which that purpose can be accomplished.

There is no necessary direction in Darwin's theory. Complexity and heterogeneity are not necessary outcomes since there is no *process* with a definite end. Natural selection acts through the complex interaction of mutation (which is *random*) and environmental change (which springs from a multiplicity of factors and which has different effects on each species). For natural selection to give rise to a necessary direction in evolution the correspondence of mutation and environmental change at all crucial conjunctures in the life of each species would have to be predetermined by the action of some cause. Clearly, that is impossible except by invoking an all-powerful deity and conjuring away the whole explanation. What appalled serious and thoughtful religious biologists about Darwin was not evolution conceived as progress, it was the *absence* of such a conception. The Darwinian system had no room at all for purpose and was ruled by the non-pre-given effects of the conjunctural combination of factors. Darwin's theory, it should be noted, is not a theory of *chance*, it is not nihilistic. Every effect or change has a determinate and explicable material cause. Each of the specific conditions is explicable by the concepts of the theory of natural selection, they stand in relation to it as particular cases of the operation of a general natural law. The particular transformations are in exactly the same relation to the general theory as particular forms of motion in given conditions are to the general laws of mechanics. Particular sequences of forms represent the action of natural selection in determinate conditions.

Darwin made use of the record of sequences of change in species and the formation of new species in the history of the earth to *illustrate* his theory and to provide support for it (he thought of it as *proof*). However, this history of the transformation of species is but one possible concrete form, other histories are possible in different conditions and in the future. The history of life on earth is but one definite case of the operation of the laws of natural selection. Darwin's theory explains that case and other possible cases stemming from different conditions because it is an abstract and general theory. It is not a generalisation from a given set of phenomena or 'facts' – if it were it would be limited to what can be derived from those facts (it would be limited to certain given conditions). Natural selection specifies a set of relations between the things it designates by its concepts (mutation of characteristics, selective pressure, etc.), and a range of possible conditions under which these relations apply. It is a general theory of the *mechanism* by which species are transformed and unlike an historical generalisation it is not confined to a given set of transformations.

Darwin did not represent his work in terms of such an epistemology. Darwin, although he was committed to an epistemology of empiricism and saw his work in the *Origin* as an induction from the facts which was to be proven by factural evidence, did not conceive his work simply as a generalisation from a history but as of general and universal significance. It was, albeit, an *hypothesis* to be constantly tried and retried against the facts, but it was not merely a description of a given case. Yet Darwin's theory has constantly been misconceived as a teleology or as a history.

4   HERBERT SPENCER

Here we will outline Spencer's conception of evolution in general and the basic nature of social evolution. It is the *form* of explanation we are interested in not the detailed content of Spencer's system. Spencer has been chosen as a representative of social evolutionary theory based upon teleology and a philosophical system because his concepts are systematic and clearly argued.

The character of progress
Spencer's social evolutionary theory is part of a *Naturphilosophie*; social evolution is but a part of the evolution of the cosmos. All nature is subject to a common evolutionary law and there is

general tendency towards progress in the cosmos. The general law of all progress is change from homogeneity to heterogeneity, the differentiation of structure and substance. Progress *is* change from the simple to the complex through differentiation. All forms of change proceed from the simple to the complex:

> The advance from the simple to the complex, through a process of successive differentiations, is seen alike in the earliest changes of the universe to which we can reason our way back; and in the earliest changes which we can inductively establish; it is seen in the geologic and climatic evolution of the earth, and in every single organism on its surface; it is seen in the evolution of Humanity . . .; it is seen in the evolution of society. [Herbert Spencer *On Social Evolution* pp. 45–6 (hereafter cited as *OSE*)]

Spencer argues that this identity of the forms of change in distinct realms of nature, the homology of the forms of progress, surely reveals that all correspond to a cosmic order, to the progress of the whole of which they are manifestations: 'And now, from this uniformity of procedure, may we not infer some fundamental necessity whence it results? May we not rationally seek some all-pervading principle which determines this all-pervading process of things? Does not the universality of the *law* imply a universal cause.' [*OSE* p. 46]

Having established the basic direction of his teleology (simple→ complex) Spencer seeks a principle that will justify and necessitate it.[1] *Why* all things tend in this direction is beyond human intelligence (the doctrine of the *Unknowable*). However, the *empirical* generalisation (things *do* change in this way) may be reduced to a *rational* generalisation, a generalisation which states the common properties of these changes in a form which accounts for and necessitates them. This generalisation, which expresses the common properties through a logical formula, is a *law*. As the common property of each of these realms is not their substance but their mode of change, this law must be a *law of change*. The law which explains the necessity of the change of things in the direction homogeneity – heterogeneity is: '*Every active force produces more than one change – every cause produces more than one effect.*' [*OSE* p. 47] Spencer supposes that this formula accounts for the tendency of the cosmos to change from the simple to the complex: 'From the law that every active force produces more than one change, it is an inevitable corollary that through all time there has been an ever-growing complication of things.' [*OSE* p. 47]

For Spencer differentiation is progress. All particular change is part of the cosmic whole: 'when we remember that the different existences with which . . . [the specialist sciences] deal are component parts of one Cosmos; we see at once that there are not several kinds of Evolution having certain units in common, but one Evolution going on everywhere in the same manner.' [*OSE* p. 72] Evolution, progress and the cosmos are, in effect, synonymous.

The nature and mechanism of social evolution

Just as the whole cosmos tends toward differentiation, social progress tends toward *individuation*. The goal of progress in the social realm is the full adaptation of man to the condition of 'civilisation' in which the individual's latent potential is realised (subject to the limits of others' freedom). 'Civilisation' is perfection – the maximisation of human happiness. Freedom in the civilised state is not anarchy; it involves mutual dependence and the division of labour which ensure the greatest variety of choice and material facilities.

Spencer's social evolutionary system involves four elements:

(i) The *goal* towards which progress tends, 'civilisation';
(ii) The *conditions* at the origin of the process, ignorance and savagery;
(iii) The *source* of change towards progress, the compulsion of population pressure;
(iv) The *mechanism* by which social advances are transmitted from stage to stage, this is Lamarckian.

The *goal* of the process and the conditions that necessitate a *process* which realises the goal are best explained in terms of Spencer's distinction between social statics and social dynamics. Spencer explains the function of these two branches of social science as follows: 'Social philosophy may be aptly divided . . . into statics and dynamics; the first treating of the equilibrium of a perfect society, the second of the forces by which society is advanced to perfection.' [*OSE* p. 17] Spencer retained the *content* of this early distinction throughout his later work. The object of statics is the definition of the goal of the social: progress in the social is the adaptation of man to the social condition. Man's perfect adaptation to this condition will result in the greatest happiness (one can clearly see here Spencer's relation to Utilitarianism). Dynamics is necessitated by man's place in the earth's evolution. Man's insertion into the cosmic process necessitates a phase of primitivism: 'the course of civilisation could not possibly have been other than it has been.' Primitivism is necessary because man must first of all conquer the earth and subordinate its creatures. Savagery is essential to this task. The primitive state of humanity creates the preconditions for civilisation, but primitivism adapts to its own savage conditions of existence and so further change is necessary to reach the social state.

Spencer explains the need for savagery in a psychologistic way. Civilised man could not kill animals except with the greatest reluctance (the civilised man takes pleasure in seeing pleasure, and feels pain at seeing pain). Savage man acquires a bloodthirsty and predatory nature (he takes pleasure in the chase and the kill) and this predatory nature cannot be limited to animals. The savage enjoys war and brutality towards his own kind: 'The treachery and vindictiveness which Bushman or Australians show to one another and to Europeans, are accompaniments of that never ceasing enmity existing between them and the denizes of the wilderness.' [*OSE* p. 19] The structure of the primitive social order is derived from the dispositions of man – these dispositions being conceived in terms of a utilitarian psychology. The dispositions are derived from the 'place' of man on earth, a 'place' defined by a philosophical conception of the cosmos.

The less adapted races of man are succeeded by the more adapted, which means, in effect, the more co-operative by the less co-operative. The slow pace of progress and the continuation of savagery within the social order serves a purpose – war, savagery directed outwards by a social group, serves to rid the earth of inferior races.

However, given man's barbarous state and his adaptation to it, why does society progress? Here we are returned to a variant of Spencer's general law of all change. Population pressure (a single cause) produces a number of effects (differentiation). Spencer utilises Malthus' law of population as the goal or stimulus to change. Population pressure forces man to improve the productivity of his means of livelihood and to reduce his fertility as a species. Increased productivity results from division of labour and co-operation – hence population pressure produces differentiation. Those who do not move in this way to escape the Malthusian trap perish. The struggle for survival promotes only those peoples who increase productivity and reduce fertility. Population pressure drives man into the social state as a form of adaptation. Population pressure is the *source* of progress: 'From the beginning pressure of population has been the proximate cause of progress . . . It forced men into the social state; made social organisation inevitable; and has developed the social sentiments . . .' [Spencer cited by Peel (1971) pp. 138–9]

Spencer's position has the effect of inverting Malthus' law of population, as Peel says: 'It is a Godwinian revenge on Malthus, Malthus turned on his head: from being the great obstacle to human perfection, the principle of population becomes its pre-requisite and guarantee.' [Peel (1971) p. 139]

It should be noted that Spencer's mutation of Malthus' principle of population bears no resemblance to the process of natural selection. Population pressure forces *cultural adaptations* and is not selection pressure acting on variant biological forms.

Spencer conceives the *mechanism* of the transmission of adaptation and evolutionary advance in a Lamarckian form. Spencer retained a Lamarckian explanation of evolutionary change in terms of the inheritance of acquired characteristics *after* the publication of Darwin's *Origin*. Larmackism was a necessary part of Spencer's theory of evolution as a cosmic process with a 'super-organic' element:

Quite apart from the biological issues raised by the debate over use-inheritance, there was a general reason why Spencer was unwilling to abandon Lamarckism – it would have driven a wedge between biological and socio-cultural or superorganic evolution, and so sullied the major premises of the entire Synthetic Philosophy. [Peel (1971) p. 143]

Evolution, conceived as a cosmic process operating through a universal law, requires a uniform causal mechanism, a mechanism applicable alike to social and biological phenomena. Transmission of acquired characteristics through *culture*, the necessary form of the transmission mechanism in social evolution, required the inheritance of acquired characteristics as the mechanism of transmission in organic evolution if the two are to be linked in one evolutionary system. Natural selection cannot embody *purpose*. Spencer cannot adopt it, if he does he must deny purpose in nature and he must separate social and biological evolution. Spencer is forced by the object and the premises of his Synthetic Philosophy to oppose

Darwin's theory. *Naturphilosophie* cannot accord explanatory autonomy to the specific natural sciences.

Spencer's social evolutionary theory and its theoretical components may be summarised as follows:

Goal	Source of evolutionary change	Mechanism of transmission
Greatest happiness through adaptation to social state	Population pressure	Inheritance acquired characteristics/ culture
Utilitarianism	*Neo-Malthusianism*	*Lamarckism*

Population pressure is the *proximate* cause of social evolution – it produces differentiation and adaptation. Yet even this cause does not have explanatory autonomy – by itself population pressure has no necessary effects; it is possible that the human species might be driven to extinction. Spencer is right to call the pressure of population a *proximate* cause. The ultimate cause of evolution as *progress* is nothing other than the general law of the evolution of all things. This 'ultimate' cause intervenes directly; it assigns man his 'place' on the earth and also the 'latent potentialities' of his nature which ensure that the outcome of the pressure of population will be a *neo*-Malthusian one and not a Malthusian one. Spencer's theory of social evolution is not separable from his Synthetic Philosophy, it is directly dependent on it. There is no 'sociological' Spencer independent of the cosmological Spencer, his conception of and classification of societies is dependent upon his philosophical system.

Evolution and history
Spencer was opposed to historical explanation and description. His teleological conception of evolution is derived from the principles of a philosophical system and not by generalisation from a history. Spencer is interested in the *process* by which progress is realised, not in history. History included all the phenomena incidental and secondary to the process, from the posturing of individuals to the King of France's nose. Knowledge of the *process* is sufficient and this knowledge is not historical. 'My position, stated briefly, is that until you have got a true theory of humanity, you cannot interpret history; and when you have got a true theory of humanity *you do*

want history.' [*OSE* p. 83] The theory of humanity determines its fundamental nature and the tendencies that arise from it. To understand humanity it is necessary to understand its role in the universe and in the general progress. This gives the true picture which is not to be found in the facts of history. To understand humanity Man must be placed in the evolution of the cosmos: 'I too, am a lover of history; but it is the history of the Cosmos as a whole. I believe you might as reasonably expect to understand the nature of the adult man by watching him for an hour . . . as to suppose that you can fathom humanity by studying the last four thousand years of its evolution.' [*OSE* p. 83] To generalise from history is to generalise from *appearances* and from a part of the whole. Man's true place is to be found in relation to the cosmos and its evolution – this evolution is not given in recent history. History is but a fragment of the general process which it is necessary to understand in order to know the evolution of humanity. Spencer's own arguments show us the difference between teleological theories of evolution and historical generalisations. *Purpose* is to be found beyond the history given to historians.

5 LEWIS HENRY MORGAN

The character of Morgan's evolutionism is radically different from Spencer's. It is not based upon a philosophical system and the content of its notion of progress is not derived from a cosmic purpose. Historical generalisation is the substance and the method of Morgan's work. *Ancient Society* is generalisation *from* a history – its division into definite successive periods; and the generalisation *of* a history – the demonstration of its universality.

The object of *Ancient Society* is conceived as a given and definite history: the sequence Savagery→Barbarism→Civilisation which is the fundamental form of the development of human society up to and into the era of recorded history. This sequence and its universality are based upon generalisation and not upon the necessity of a teleological process impelled towards a definite end. This sequence *is* the way that human society developed, this can be shown by investigation of the historical record and by generalisation from other kinds of evidence. For Morgan, what Spencer derides as 'the last four thousand years' of humanity's development is the primary object of analysis. In *Ancient Society* the cosmos has no place: its object is the specific history of man.

The sequence Savagery→Barbarism→Civilisation is not haphazard or accidental. History happened *this* way and it could not have happened otherwise. This history is determined by the character of the human mind. The human mind, its uniform character throughout the species and its development with man's development, explains the universality of this history and the fact that it followed a common pattern:

> This fact [the common sequence of development in different cultures] forms part of the accumulating evidence tending to show that the principal institutions of mankind have been developed from a few primary germs of thought; and the course and manner of their development was predetermined, as well as restricted within narrow limits of divergence, by the natural logic of the human mind and the necessary limitation of its powers. [*Ancient Society* p. 18]

In the first period of savagery man's mental nature and the conditions he faced were common to all races and cultures; the primary *germs* of thought were, therefore, common too. These germs of all subsequent development reflected the common problems confronting savage life and their common origin in the mind of savage man. The human mind developed with the process of social development, the brain grew with the inventions and institutions it engendered:

> With the production of inventions and discoveries, the human mind necessarily grew and expanded; and we are led to recognise a gradual enlargement of the brain itself, particularly of the cerebral portion. The slowness of this mental growth was inevitable, in the period of savagery, from the extreme difficulty of compassing the simplest invention out of nothing, or with next to nothing to assist mental effort; and of discovering any substance or force in nature available in such a rude condition of life. [*Ancient Society* p. 36]

In referring to the 'human mind' Morgan does not mean the minds of particular individuals but the mental labours of organised groups and of the species as a whole:

> It fortunately so happens that the events of human progress embody themselves, independently of particular men, in a material

B

record, which is crystallised in institutions, usages and customs, and preserved in inventions and discoveries . . . The work of society in its totality, by means of which all progress occurs, is ascribed too much to individual men, and far too little to the public intelligence. It will be recognised generally that the substance of human history is bound up in the growth of ideas, which are brought out by the people and expressed in their institutions, usages, inventions and discoveries. [*Ancient Society* p. 311]

While this history could not have had a different pattern it was neither necessary nor inevitable that man's development should have proceeded through its various stages. The sequence of Savagery, Barbarism and Civilisation is not a function of some teleological evolutionary 'law' which prescribes a definite end or purpose for mankind. This process is a given history; although it could not have happened other than it did, it was not necessary that it happened as it did, it was not necessary that man progress beyond any given stage. 'Progress' for Morgan is the actual process of development itself – it is what is actually accomplished in that process. Morgan brings no cosmic purpose or ethical system to the measure of 'progress'. Progress is whatever mankind has successively accomplished.

The final stage of the succession of periods in *Ancient Society*, 'Civilisation', is not *final* – civilisation is not an end. 'Civilisation' begins with writing, it includes the post-Homeric Greeks. 'Civilisation' is not the modern West, but all those cultures which have attained writing and the other concomitant skills. Man's development is not completed. The family and government are still developing:

When the fact is accepted that the family has passed through four successive forms, and is now in a fifth, the question at once arises whether this form can be permanent in the future. The only answer that can be given is, that it must advance as society advances, and change as society changes, even as it has done in the past. [*Ancient Society* p. 499]

and:

The nature of the coming changes it may be impossible to conceive; but it seems probable that democracy, once universal in a rudimentary form and repressed in many civilised states, is destined to become again universal and supreme. [*Ancient Society* p. 357]

It is a history to which Morgan addresses himself, not the closed inevitability of a teleological process. There is no 'necessary future' in *Ancient Society*, no pre-given end to history. The history of man is a *fact*, it need not have occurred:

> When we recognise the duration of man's existence upon the earth, the wide vicissitudes through which he has passed in savagery and barbarism, and the progress he was compelled to make, civilisation might as naturally have been delayed for several thousand years in the future, as to have occurred when it did in the good providence of God . . . It may well serve to remind us that we owe our present condition, with its multiplied means of safety and of happiness, to the struggles, the sufferings, the heroic exertions and the patent toil of our barbarous, and more remotely, of our savage ancestors. [*Ancient Society* p. 563]

This history is made by the struggles of men, not by a process or as the effect of a 'law'. History is a process with a subject; that subject is humanity. History is the development *of* something, of mankind and his creative powers. History is not a simple fact, it has a meaning, a positive content. Morgan's conception of history places him squarely within one of the main branches of historicism.

History for Morgan is the history of 'invention and discovery', and of the development of the 'ideas' of institutional forms. It is a history of the successive transformations effected by the products of Man's mind, of innovation through the effects of invention. Several 'ideas' are formed and developed in the human mind: the 'ideas' of government, of the family and of property. These 'ideas' develop as successive forms. 'Invention' and 'discovery' which have their origin in the human mind are used by Morgan to explain the successive 'ethnical periods' and the advances in man's condition of life associated with them. This reference to 'invention' and the development of the 'ideas' is the explanation of the sequences Morgan establishes by generalisation from the facts of history.

Morgan was *not*, contrary to the popular misconception, a materialist: 'It is accordingly probable that the great epochs of human progress have been *identified*, more or less directly, with the enlargement of the sources of subsistence.' [*Ancient Society* p. 19 (my emphasis)] He argues that the 'arts of subsistence' are 'identified' with certain definite periods of advance, not that they were *determined* or *caused* by them. Subsistence is expanded and developed by new techniques and inventions and enlarged means of subsistence create cultural possibilities. However, the 'arts of subsistence' are effects of 'invention', of the human mind. Subsistence is a factor the importance of which varies; it is less significant at the later stages ('intelligence from henceforth becomes a more prominent factor', p. 20) and more important at the earlier stages when man is closer to the animals. The development of the human mind, the progressive improvement of its inventions, frees man from the grip of necessity and assigns the task of finding something to eat to a secondary place.

Morgan must not be reduced to Engels' *reading* of Morgan. Engels' *Origin of the Family, Private Property and the State* is more often read than *Ancient Society*. It *uses* Morgan rather than summarises him. In the *Origin* Engels uses Morgan's analysis of the development of the 'ideas' of the family and of government; he inserts the successive institutional forms presented by Morgan into his own discourse and uses them to illustrate the problems he, and not Morgan, raises in that text. The explanatory system used in the *Origin* is not Morgan's idealistic and mentalistic one but that of historical materialism. Engels himself noted in the *Origin*: 'the forms of the changes are, in the main, described by Morgan: the economic content which gave rise to them I had largely to add myself.'

In Morgan's work there is no trace of a theory of historical materialism. In *Ancient Society* there is a definite theory of the correspondence of the levels of development of the different 'ideas'; distinct complexes of forms of the family, of government, of subsistence, etc., form social totalities. There is no hierarchy of determinance between the different 'ideas' or their forms. The family is not more significant in the totality than, say, the form of government. The totalities are *descriptive*; the correspondences of institutional forms are given facts. The various correspondences are an effect of the general level of development of the human mind in a particular ethnical period and of particular forms of institutional interrelationship, thus certain family forms are prerequisites for certain forms of government. These totalities are also variable in their content within a given period; the correspondences involved are not essential, there can be systematic discrepancies in the level of development of different institutional forms within the same society. In Morgan's *Ancient Society* the form of the social totality is the more or less systematic correspondence of institutional forms which are equivalent in their importance. The precise nature of the correspondence and of the forms is an empirical matter. Morgan does not have a theory of the social totality as a necessary structure with a definite hierarchy of forms and causes. Morgan's general conception of the social totality necessarily refers to the particular; its content is provided by the description of the actual forms of concrete societies.

Morgan differs from Engels' position: Engels does have a definite general concept of the necessary structure of all social totalities, and this structure is a hierarchy of determinations. Engels' position in the *Origin* is best represented by Marx's 1859 Preface to *A Contribution to the Critique of Political Economy*. In this text the economy is assigned the role of the *structure* in the social totality which forms the *foundation* for a political–legal *superstructure*, to which *correspond* definite forms of social consciousness. This metaphor of structure and superstructure assigns a necessary determining role to the economic level of the social totality. Although the superstructure is not reduced to a direct economic causation, it is limited by the *foundation* which is its condition of existence and which assigns it its limits. Further, the forms of social consciousness *correspond* to this superstructure – they are secondary or subordinate forms. The correspondence argued for in the 1859 Preface is quite different from the correspondence/equivalence of each of the major institutions in *Ancient Society*. Historical materialism excludes the determining or originative role Morgan assigns to 'invention' and 'ideas'.

The social totalities in each of Morgan's 'ethnical periods' are descriptive; they are the actual forms of concrete societies and are quite unlike Marx's concept of distinct 'modes of production'. The concept of 'ethnical period' is itself a descriptive one. These periods are formed by identifying the dominant forms in different eras. They are supposed to be an empirical division of history into its dominant real forms. The ethnical periods, products of generalisation from the facts, form a classificatory system; they define levels of development by reference to certain concrete human achievements. The succession of periods represents the history of human development, each of the periods first comes into being at a definite time and has its era of dominance. The history of human development is formed by generalisation, linking together the successive advances made by different peoples. This 'history' generalises and reconstructs a succession of forms, it is a single and a universal history. A *single* history: Savagery, Barbarism and Civilisation is a sequence that occurs *once* in history, it occurs when peoples first progress to Barbarism and then to Civilisation. A *universal* history: this sequence is repeated as other peoples first progress to Barbarism and then to Civilisation. It is not an *inevitable* history: peoples may remain at given stages. The dominance of an ethnical period does not prevent the coexistence of forms from other periods. Thus 'ethnical periods' refer at one and the same time to successive divisions of a general human history and to forms of social totality which may coexist with others of a different period.

The classificatory system of *Ancient Society* is organised around the succession of concrete institutions, inventions and customs, and is not based upon principles like the universal movement from homogeneity to heterogeneity. The classificatory system does not have the completeness of a plan or series (history is not finished), nor are its forms *types* (we have seen that Morgan's conception of the social totality is loose and descriptive). The classification resembles those of history or archaeology rather than those of evolutionary teleology or systematic morphology. Its essence is the breaking of a given past into periods, breaks based on the concrete forms found in these periods. However, it should not be thought that this apparently 'descriptive' classification is empirical and, therefore, superior to those of Cuvier or Spencer. It is not empirical, it is *empiricist*. The 'facts' it orders are given this status, selected and ordered by implicit criteria. These criteria are hidden in the process of selection, they are neither conceptualised nor rationally defended. In this Morgan does indeed resemble history and archaeology.

The practice of systematic generalisation which divides the whole of human history into distinct ethnical periods rests upon certain assumptions:

(i) That man's nature is essentially uniform – this uniformity is a function of the identical nature of the brain in all the different races of mankind (*see* p. 8 in *Ancient Society*).

(ii) That in similar conditions men think and act in a similar way. Thus one can deduce from the customs and institutions of existing non-civilised peoples the conditions of man at periods when an earlier level of development predominated:

> The remote ancestors of the Aryan nations *presumptively* passed through an experience similar to that of existing barbarous and savage tribes . . . [their experience anterior to civilisation and the highest stage of Barbarism] . . . must be *deduced* in the main from the traceable connection between the elements of their existing institutions and inventions, and similar elements preserved in those of savage and and barbarous tribes. [*Ancient Society* pp. 7–8 (my emphasis)]

and:

> So essentially identical are the arts, institutions and mode of life in the same status upon all the continents, that the archaic form of the principal domestic institutions of the Greeks and Romans must even now be sought in the corresponding institutions of the American aborigines. [*Ancient Society* p. 17]

(iii) That similar institutions in widely different regions, while registering the influence of environments, reveal the unity of the ethnical periods (*see* pp. 16–17 of *Ancient Society*).

There are three main methods of reconstructing the previously dominant levels of Savagery and Barbarism:

(i) The evidence of previous stages revealed in the institutions of a higher level – this is an effect of the uneven development of the different levels and the fact that the mode of expression of institutional forms changes *after* the institution changes;

(ii) Generalisation ('presumptively,' cf. *Ancient Society* p. 7) from currently existing barbarous and savage peoples to the institutions in the periods when savagery and barbarism predominated;

(iii) The analysis of the lower stages of Savagery by the abstraction of the elements of the higher stages and the logical deduction of the conditions which would prevail in the absence of these elements.

Ethnical periods are therefore constituted by means of rules for the generalisation of evidence from one case to another and by logical deductions based upon the assumption of uniform effects in uniform conditions.

The 'progress' revealed in the successive ethnical periods and which justifies them being considered as levels of advance is not some principle or ethical ideal – its content is descriptive and deductive. 'Progress' is nominal – it is nothing other than what is accomplished, the successive inventions and institutions which appear in each ethnical period. 'Progress' has no content other than the concrete forms in which it is measured.

Morgan demonstrates the contribution of each period to human 'progress' by working backwards through history and excluding the institutions and inventions which first appear in each period – the effect of this is to diminish progressively the powers and comforts available to man. The contribution of the different ethnical periods to man's culture is not equivalent, nor does 'progress' proceed in a simple ascending scale. The greatest contribution to man's mode of life and the most dramatic leap forward is made in the period of Barbarism: 'If mankind had never advanced beyond this condition, they had the means of an easy and enjoyable life.' [*Ancient Society* p. 42] Civilisation is but a superstructure erected on the heroic achievements of Barbarism.

Morgan's sequence of ethnical periods is not 'unilinear', it does not prescribe a course which all peoples must inevitably follow. Morgan allowed for the *diffusion* of arts of subsistence, 'ideas' of government, etc., from one people to another. Not all peoples have followed or will follow this sequence which is the general sequence of human history. Morgan does not consider Savages and Barbarians contemporary with the civilised world as *anachronisms* or 'left-overs'. The Iroquois are a social organisation in their own right, not a survival. Savages and Barbarians are being extinguished through conquest and transformed through civilisation; this is a simple *fact*, not an inevitable process. The fate of the Iroquois is circumstantial, the ending of the dominance of Barbarism by the appearance of Civilisation in the Americas, and not inevitable.

Social evolutionary thinkers are often charged with a conjectural and cavalier attitude to concrete social relations. Morgan is usually lumped with Spencer and McLennan in this respect. However, Morgan exemplifies the different ethnical periods by reference to the social institutions of distinct peoples functioning as a totality; to the Iroquois, the ancient Greeks and Romans, etc. His generalisations are not supported in the manner of Spencer or McLennan by random examples of individual institutions and customs abstracted from the social relations in which they existed. In this sense Morgan's work had a definite ethnographic basis. It is his generalisations, from the institutions of one people to another, and to earlier forms of a culture from existent forms, which aroused the criticism and hostility of relativists and functionalists. Whatever the character of Morgan's ethnography, his project would inevitably have led to a conflict with the Boas school.

It should be noted that for a thinker who is considered a 'social evolutionist' Morgan makes very little use of the notions of *adaptation* or *variation*. Invention is not an adaptive process and Morgan does not introduce environmental change or population pressure as a general explanatory mechanism. Invention brings an increase in security and comfort but it is not adaptive change; beyond the most primitive levels of Savagery man has all the necessary elements of a satisfactory life. It was not environmental necessity but the human mind which took man beyond the primitive state. Morgan considers the higher stages of human society to be more fully endowed with inventions, techniques and institutional forms, but, beyond the most primitive stages, the 'higher' forms are not different in nature from the lower ones. Morgan has no social morphology based upon the axis of simplicity and complexity like Spencer or Durkheim. There are in *Ancient Society* no antitheses like Gemeinschaft/Gesellschaft, Mechanical and Organic Solidarity, and so on. There are no radical changes in the quality of social organisation; all human societies from the most simple to the most complicated are emanations of a common human nature. Social organisation changes in form and degree but not in essence.

This discussion has concentrated on Morgan's method and the nature of his reconstruction of human history. It has two objectives: to separate Morgan from the familiar image of the archetypal unilinear evolutionist; to separate his method and conception of history from that of Marx and Engels. Both of these objectives require qualification. It should not be thought that in differentiating Morgan's position from teleological evolutionisms we are arguing that it is epistemologically superior to them. Although Morgan's theory is not teleological in the sense that Spencer's is, it is teleological in another sense, that it ascribes history to the human mind. History is unified as the product of that mind and is the development of that mind's potentialities. Morgan differs from Spencer principally in that he does not seek to necessitate development in a superhistorical cause, to make history a necessary process. The differentiation of Morgan's method from Marx's should not be construed as a rejection of Morgan *tout court*. One aspect of Morgan's work remains of lasting, and neglected, value to Marxism: his conception of the social organisation of ancient society in terms of the Gentile Constitution. Barry Hindess and I have argued the significance of this concept for the Marxist theory of the state and the analysis of so-called 'primitive' societies in another work (Hindess & Hirst, 1975, ch. 1). Morgan's significance is, however, not that attributed to him by orthodox Marxism. Furthermore, Morgan's loose conception of the social totality means that it is possible to separate his concept of the Gentile Constitution from his more dubious notions about the evolution of forms of the family without serious contradiction. Orthodox Marxism has, however, treated his work as a consistent whole, coincident with Marxism, and to be defended *in toto*.

7   TERRAY, MORGAN AND HISTORICAL MATERIALISM

In *Marxism and 'Primitive Societies'* Emmanuel Terray presents a new variant of the orthodox Marxist defence of Morgan. This defence does not attempt to save particular aspects of Morgan's theory, such as the succession of forms of the family accepted by Engels and challenged by modern anthropology. Terray's defence consists in arguing that Morgan independently produced central elements of Marx's theory of historical materialism. Terray supposes he is vouchsafed the scientificity of Marxism by the philosophy of Althusser. We will challenge this attempt to demonstrate a correspondence between Morgan's work and historical materialism.

Terray's object in the essay 'Morgan and Contemporary Anthropology' is to demonstrate that Morgan's theory is similar in certain crucial respects to that of Marx. The most important elements of this correspondence are the following: Morgan's object, like Marx's, is to construct a system of general concepts that will make a scientific analysis of history possible, and Morgan conceives the structure of the social totality in a fundamentally similar way to Marx – ascribing a determining role to the economy. Morgan and Marx have their primary object and certain crucial concepts in common. Because of the identity of the two problematics in these two fundamental respects Morgan's analyses and conclusions can be incorporated into the body of Marxist theory. Engels' *Origin* is not merely a *reading* of Morgan's work which annexes Morgan's analyses to its own concepts and for its own ends, it is rather a legitimate translation of an analogous position into a clear and more rigorous system of concepts.

Here we shall question the two most important aspects of this correspondence of Marx and Morgan:

(i) That they have the same *object* – to analyse history by means of general concepts;
(ii) That they have the same basic conception of social totality.

How does Terray argue for this correspondence between Morgan's and Marx's theories? He does so by attempting to show the parallelism of certain concepts; to show that Morgan's concept must mean the same as Marx's. Firstly, Terray argues that a 'Darwinist' reading of Morgan is possible; that is, that Morgan applied the concepts of biological evolutionism to the study of society (concepts such as the transformation of forms, natural selection, etc.). Terray attempts to demonstrate these affinities with Darwin by a series of correspondences of terms in certain passages of Morgan with evolutionist terms. Correspondence is at the level of terminology and 'themes'. Terray does not attempt to examine and compare rigorously the two *theories* in question (Morgan's and Darwin's), relating the manifest terms and 'themes' to the system of concepts which defines the theoretical content of the texts in question. The difference of the objects of these two theories (Darwin – a general theory of the mechanism of transformation of animal species; Morgan – a general history of mankind's development) or of their explanatory mechanisms (Darwin – natural selection; Morgan – invention) is not registered. Having established these apparent correspondences Terray argues that they are merely similarities. In fact Morgan's work is not reducible to 'Darwinism' because a residue of non-Darwinian concepts and problems remains.[2]

Terray reveals the arbitrariness of his method by the manner in which he overcomes this question of similarity *v.* correspondence. Why is Morgan not a social Darwinist? The irreducibility of Morgan's theory to Darwinism is established by an appeal to authority. Marx and Engels opposed the application of 'principles' (supposedly) derived from Darwin to human history. They criticise such applications (by Lange, Lavrov, etc.) as reductions of

Darwin's explanatory mechanism to a slogan (e.g. 'the struggle for existence') which is simply imposed on all and any phenomena. But Marx and Engels had the highest opinion of Morgan. Engels said that Morgan had 'spontaneously discovered Marx's materialist conception of history'. Terray comments: 'Such penetrating readers as Marx and Engels can be *trusted*: an alternative reading of *Ancient Society* is possible.' [Terray (1972) p. 23 (my emphasis)] Engels said so, therefore it is true! It is true because Engels can be *trusted*. That Marx and Engels might be radically wrong about Morgan and the nature of their relation to him is never raised because it is never even considered. The problems of arbitrariness are overcome with arbitrariness.

Having assumed the validity of Engels' interpretation, Terray sets out to show how Morgan's work really does correspond to historical materialism.

(i) *Science and history*

Morgan's *object* marks him off from all pseudo-Darwinists who merely vulgarise already existing concepts and use them to explain given facts. Morgan's theory cannot be reduced to a mere borrowing from Darwin because it sets out to do something which requires original concepts, something which is inconceivable except in the terms of those concepts. Morgan's object is: *not* 'to describe the different stages of human social evolution, or to write a history of humanity, but to construct a *theory* of that history, that is, a system of concepts which make it possible to think it out scientifically.' [Terray (1972) p. 24]

Terray attempts to prove that it *is* an abstract and scientific theory using general concepts (that is, concepts which are not abstractions from or generalisation of 'facts') which Morgan constructs. We shall challenge this and support the validity of our own explanations – that Morgan's concepts are abstractions and generalisations from the 'facts' of what is supposed to be a given history.

Terray attempts to demonstrate that *Ancient Society* is not a history and that it involves general concepts by reference to Morgan's notion of 'form'. Terray takes the 'forms' to be examples of general concepts; they are general concepts because their content is not reducible to particular given facts. The 'forms' of the family or of government are not the same as particular concrete political or family institutions. The succession of forms is not equivalent to the succession of events in particular histories.

Terray uses the notion of 'history' to mean a narrative or chronicle of a succession of events. Terray has so defined history that any attempt to write a *general* history, a history of more than one people, a history above the level of a chronicle, must appear to be a general theory. Terray in using the distinction between the 'forms' and concrete events does not consider that Morgan's own description of the 'forms' as 'hypotheses' might be a strictly accurate one. Morgan's 'forms' are *abstractions* from concrete events; generalisations in which the essence of many concrete 'facts' is summarised, and generalisations which are *generalised* to cover other 'facts'. All Terray shows is that Morgan is not an ultra-empiricist who believes that knowledge is confined to the description of particular cases. Morgan's method is that of a form of positivism: *abstraction* – selection from the 'facts'; *generalisation* – the formation of 'hypotheses'; and the *proof* of the hypotheses by their extension to new facts. It is not abstract theory but empiricist abstraction. There is a very real difference between an abstract and general theory, derived from and reducible to no specific set of observables, the type of theory exemplified by Darwin's explanation of speciation, and a theory, however complex and wide ranging, which claims to be a generalisation from certain given facts, events, or cases.

Terray simply fails to consider any other possible explanations of Morgan's epistemology than the crudest empiricism. Having shown that Morgan is not an ultra-empiricist he assumes he is a scientific theorist. An example of this is his attitude to teleology: 'It is most significant that there is no *élan vital*, necessarily metaphysical, such as would compel a particular real society to progress from one 'form' . . . to another, and to go through all the steps in the "sequence" of progress.' [Terray (1972) p. 30] This is quite true, but to claim that Morgan's work is historical generalisation accounts for this just as well as the claim that *Ancient Society* is a work of general scientific theory. Furthermore, it is a misleading truth. Indeed, Morgan's history is rendered necessary by no 'purpose', but it is rendered coherent and explained teleologically by reference to the 'human mind'.

Later in his essay Terray admits that Morgan 'remained prisoner of an empiricist ideology of knowledge' (p. 38), but it does not seem to concern him that he has used this very 'ideology' to show that Morgan is a general theorist. Having shown that Morgan claims to be an empiricist or positivist Terray assumes there is a discrepancy between his representation of his position and his actual position. There is no justification for this whatever, since, as we have seen, Terray's claims for *abstractness* are justified by examples that point to *abstraction*. Terray simply fails to argue *why* these examples cannot be considered as examples of a positivist method. The validity of Terray's interpretation is again justified by appeal to authority. Firstly, to Alain Badiou – to tell us that Marx's theory was quite different from empiricism. Secondly, to Marx, thus fortified – to tell us that Marx could not have approved of Morgan if he was an empiricist or positivist: 'The reason for Marx's admiration of Morgan must, therefore, be sought in other aspects of Morgan's work.' [Terray (1972) p. 39]

(ii) *The structure of the social totality*

The 'other aspects' of Marx's appreciation of Morgan are to be found in his supposed duplication of the fundamental explanatory mechanism of historical materialism; the determination of the social totality by its economic structure. Terray argues that Morgan assigns a *determining* function to the 'arts of subsistence' (Terray p. 52). To demonstrate this he cites various passages from *Ancient Society*. These passages prove nothing. In stating the relation between the 'arts of subsistence' and other social forms Morgan uses the notions of 'influence' (p. 9) and 'identification' (p. 19) to describe the nature of this relation. These notions in no way *say* that the relation is a relation of determination nor can a determining role be assigned to the 'arts . . .' from the context in which these notions are used. All Terray does in citing these passages is to show that Morgan assigns *some* effectivity to the 'arts . . .', that they have a certain influence on other social relations rather than none at all. Given Morgan's loose and descriptive conception of the social totality and the absence of any rigorous hierarchy of determination in it, it is inevitable that the 'arts . . .' should have a definite influence and effect. Terray fails to argue against other conceptions of Morgan's theory, in particular he fails to deal with Morgan's claim that the 'arts . . .' become *less* significant with the development of the public intelligence.

Terray's attempt to demonstrate Morgan's affinity with historical materialism involves him in the assumption that the 'arts of subsistence' are equivalent to Marx's 'economic structure of society'. By 'arts of subsistence' Morgan means the material instruments and techniques by which food and other necessaries are obtained. By 'economic structure' Marx designates a complex combination of the forces and the social relations of production, that is, material production takes place through and by means of definite social relations. The social relations of production provide the conditions of material reproduction (through a definite social distribution of the means of production) and constitute the form of distribution of the product (as a function of the distribution of the means of production). Production presupposes not only techniques but also a property/possession connection. The character of the product and its distribution are determined by the social relations of production; these relations enforce a definite distribution of the means of production, a social division of labour corresponding to this distribution which assigns specific functions to the agents of production (worker, capitalist, functionary, etc.), and, as a consequence of this distribution and division, a specific distribution of the product between the categories of agents of production. In Marx's concept of 'economic structure', therefore, the technical means of production are connected to a definite social structure. The notion of the 'arts of subsistence' does not correspond to this combination of forces and relations of production since the 'arts . . .' explicitly exclude the 'idea' of property and, therefore, the social relations of distribution. Morgan has no concept equivalent to the 'social relations of production'.

The only basis on which the 'arts . . .' could be equivalent to 'economic structure' is in a technological determinist variant of Marxism in which the economy is in effect reduced to the techniques of production. In this, a part of Morgan's multi-factorial theory of history would correspond to a theory of history dominated by a single factor. Yet even the most cryptic and economistic passages of the 1859 Preface never permit a consistent interpretation of Marxism as a technological determinism. The sole condition on which Terray can achieve even a limited correspondence of Marx and Morgan is to reduce Marx's theory to the crude 'materialistic interpretation of history' that led Marx in disgust to say 'I am not a Marxist'.

The key to our problematisation of the notion of 'evolutionism' has been the concept of teleology. The non-teleological theory of natural selection was contrasted with theories in the biological and social sciences which subject all nature to a universal principle producing purposive change, and with the practice of reconstructing by generalisation specific successions of biological and social forms. In the next chapter a different kind of teleology will play its part.

Central to Weber's sociology is the teleology of human wills; society is the product of meaningful inter-subjective action. Although the explanations and classifications produced by Spencer and Weber are strikingly different in content, scope and appearance, both are limited as theoretical discourses by their commitment to purpose; Spencer is condemned to a vacuous pan-scientism, and Weber to radical relativism. This connection between the two examples chosen will be further developed in the conclusion.

3

Weber's Sociological Categories

Economy and Society was Max Weber's attempt to provide a system of categories which could serve as guides to empirical sociological analysis. Weber's categories have been so used. The majority of sociologists working on questions of politics, economics, law or religion probably regard Weber's categories and types as the best means of organisation and classification of their fields currently available. The general thesis of this book is that classifications of social forms are dependent on and products of specific social theories. Weber's classifications and categories are no exception. In the following chapters we will specifically concern ourselves with Weber's types of legitimate domination and sociological categories of economic action as presented in *Economy and Society*. It will be argued that these classifications and categories are a part of theoretical discourse. The logical consistency of this discourse and implications of these categories for the analysis of social relations will be considered.

Weber's categories form the basis of so much of modern sociological work on political and economic questions because they are the main alternative to or substitute for the theories of Marx. It will be argued that, far from providing a rigorous classification of and means of analysis of forms of state and political rule, the Weberian types mystify 'domination'. The definition of the types as forms of legitimation of rule obscures the conditions, apparatuses and instruments of political rule. The Weberian problem of legitimacy displaces the questions of the structure of the state and its social conditions of existence; objective social relations are dissolved into the inter-subjective relation of master and subordinate. 'Domination' is conceived by Weber as an inter-subjective relationship; legitimacy becomes the key problem in this theory of politics because power depends on compliance, rule based on force could not long survive. However, the conditions of compliance of the subordinate subject are abolished by Weber's categories; in fact all stable forms of rule are presumed to evoke the *de facto* obedience of the governed in the forms required by their rulers. Stability *is* legitimacy. Whether subjects obey freely or not, how and why they obey, is of no consequence. 'Domination' exists wherever subjects obey the commands of other subjects, the conditions of existence of forms of rule disappear into the inter-subjective relation of command and obedience. Obedience provides its own conditions; in the act of obedience is to be found the origin and foundation of the state. Popular democratic institutions are excluded as possible forms of rule by Weber's categories.

Weber's three types are not 'one-sided accentuations' of reality, as it supposed in *Economy and Society* – they have nothing whatever to do with 'reality' but are products of theoretical discourse. In order to understand these categories it is necessary to know something about the knowledge process in which they are supposed to function. For this reason it will be necessary to begin with a long digression, a discussion of the Weberian epistemology and theory of social action. Weber's epistemology cannot be taken for granted since it is the subject of some dispute.

In the same texts as he presents his sociological categories Weber conducts a polemic against democracy and socialism. Democratic forms of rule are impossible. Economic relations are conceived in such a way that capitalist production and exchange are the only 'rational' forms of economy. Socialism is possible as an economic system only as an inferior and less rational copy of the main elements of capitalism within a rigid state bureaucratic system.

We will examine the three types of domination, the sociological categories of economic action, and the polemical attack on popular democracy in separate chapters.

WEBER'S EPISTEMOLOGY

Weber's epistemological position may be characterised as 'neo-Kantian positivism'. What does this mean? We use this term in a specific sense, to refer to the introduction of positivistic methods and problems into the spiritual/cultural sciences tradition (*Geisteswissenschaften*). The neo-Kantian distinction of nature and culture as realms of mechanical causality, on the one hand, and teleological causality, on the other, is combined with the positivistic nominalisation of the categories and results of knowledge. Thus Weber unifies a 'cultural scientific' conception of the object of historical/social knowledge with a positivist conception of the nature and methods of empirical knowledge.

This combination involves the rejection of elements of both positivism and cultural idealism. Culture is a specific object. The cultural sciences do not aim to construct general laws as do the natural sciences, the phenomena of culture are unique and not subject to generalisation. Culture consists in meanings produced by human subjects, and is governed by a causality of purpose. The cultural sciences must 'understand' the significance of these meanings if they are to know cultural phenomena. Objective knowledge in the realm of culture must respect the nature of its object; there can be no simple transference of the methods of the natural sciences.

Classical positivism's insistence that the sciences are unified by a common method, that the divisions of the sciences are conventional, *within* knowledge, and not essential differences in being, is denied by neo-Kantian positivism. The difference between the natural and the cultural realms is an essential ontological difference; neo-Kantian positivism involves a definite metaphysics. But if the object of knowledge is essentialised, knowledge of it is nominalised. Neo-Kantian positivism rejects the epistemological positions hitherto dominant in the cultural sciences, objective idealism and subjectivism, and it does so on the basis of positivist method. It rejects the certainty of objective idealist knowledge. Empirical knowledge is limited and provisional, it is not and never can be knowledge of the essence of things, whether cultural or physical. This form of neo-Kantianism extends the nominalism of positivism into the realm of culture. Cultural 'phenomena' are given facts with no necessary or visible interconnections. Relations between cultural phenomena must be established by investigation. The relations thus established are products of the operations of knowledge and as such cannot be final; the categories of knowledge applied to cultural facts and the constructions placed upon them are provisional and subject to verification. On the other hand, it rejects the limitations of subjectivist knowledge. In the realm of culture knowledge is not introspective or intuitive, but objective. The cultural sciences like the natural sciences require methods of investigation which demonstrate the validity of propositions by reference to *what is*.

Our point of departure in considering Weber's epistemology is the collection of essays *The Methodology of the Social Sciences*. We will present an analytic summary of Weber's position in these essays and then subject it to critical commentary. Later, the relation of the essays to *Economy and Society* will be considered. Weber's epistemo-logical position starts from the fundamental neo-Kantian division of the natural and the cultural sciences. Following Heinrich Rickert, Weber argues that objective knowledge is possible in the cultural sciences, that the knower is not condemned to be purely subjective and evaluative because the object of his knowledge is a realm of values. Weber accepts Rickert's distinction between *evaluation* (*Wertung*) and *value-relatedness* (*Wertbeziehung*). The selection of the pheno-mena to be studied and the point of view from which they are studied is not merely subjective and arbitrary – phenomena are selected and studied in terms of their significance for supra-individual cultural values. The significance of an object does not stem from the fact that the knower personally values it but because he seeks its relatedness to cultural values. Value-relatedness makes possible the determination of the *cultural significance* of events, persons and ideas. Unlike Rickert, however, Weber rejects the notion that there are universal objective values in terms of which cultural significance can be assessed. Cultural significance must be established relative to specific value systems, systems which are in competition with others. In denying the validity of universal values Weber is forced to find another basis for the cultural sciences. He found the unity of the cultural sciences on the human subject as a being creating values and projecting them into the world:

> The transcendental presupposition of every *cultural science* lies not in our finding a certain culture or any 'culture' in general to be valuable but rather in the fact that we are *cultural beings*, endowed with the capacity and the will to take a definite attitude toward the world and to lend it *significance*. [*Methodology* p. 81 (emphasis in the original)]

Weber contends that this basis of the uniqueness and the unity of the object of the cultural sciences is a '*transcendental pre-supposition*'; a metaphysical assumption of the uniqueness of culture which cannot be proven or disproven by the methods of empirical knowledge. Culture is a unique object because of the unique attri-butes of the being which creates it, will and purpose. Weber is com-mitted to a positive anthropology prior to the operations of knowledge in the 'cultural sciences': in the presupposed ontology of the subject is presupposed the whole nature and content of the cultural realm. Weber's knowledge of the social starts with the supposition of the human subject as a free being.

Relatedness-to-values determines the phenomena selected for study and the problems of analysis in terms of which these phenomena are significant:

> . . . the expression 'relevance to values' refers simply to the philosophical interpretation of that specifically scientific 'interest' which *determines* the selection of a *given subject matter and the problems of an empirical analysis.*
> In empirical investigation, no 'practical evalutions' are legitimated by this strictly logical fact. But together with historical experience, it shows that *cultural (i.e. evaluative) interests give purely scientific work its direction.* [*Methodology* p. 22 (my emphasis)]

Only through 'cultural interests' is it possible to select between the infinite diversity of events and individuals which characterises the cultural realm; social life represents '. . . an infinite multiplicity of successively and coexistently emerging and disappearing events.' [*Methodology* p. 72] Selection from this infinity is necessary in order that knowledge has a definite object: 'All the analysis of infinite reality which the finite human mind can conduct rests upon the tacit assumption that only a finite portion of this reality constitutes the object of scientific investigation, and that only it is "important" in the sense of being "worthy of being known".' [*Methodology* p. 72] Without a prior and non-empirical definition of the objects and problems of investigation, empirical knowledge is blind. Values are necessary to reach the concrete, to recognise its individuality by knowing its cultural significance. For Weber, relatedness-to-values is not a preconception which is an obstacle to knowledge, a valuation which distorts the facts: it is the precondition of empirical knowledge in the realm of culture, a special form of valuation which makes it possible to study the facts of culture.

It should be noted that the insistence of positivism on the separation of statements of fact and valuations does not prevent the positivistic study of values. Positivism claims to be a *method* and not a legislative metaphysics; it does not deny that values *exist*, rather it merely asserts that they cannot enter into the content of empirical knowledge. If it is possible to study values 'objectively' and to subject propositions made about them to criteria of empirical proof, then according to positivist criteria of scientificity, the study of values can be 'scientific'.

Weber attempts to retain the positivist separation of statements of fact and value-judgements in a strict form. That the object of knowledge is a realm of values does not mean that the *personal* values of the knowing subject need enter into the process of empirical knowledge. Relatedness-to-values is established *prior* to and *subsequent* to the process of empirical knowledge. Cultural scientific knowledge, in so far as it is empirical knowledge, can only know the phenomena of the cultural world through the intervention of and relative to a definite value system; it cannot choose between such systems: 'An empirical science cannot tell anyone what he *should* do – but rather what he *can* do – and under certain circumstances – what he wishes to do.' [*Methodology* p. 54 (emphasis in the original)] Empirical knowledge must always find the objects and purposes of its knowledge given to it: 'Strictly and exclusively empirical analysis can provide a solution only where it is a question of the means adequate to an absolutely unambiguously given end.' [*Methodology* p. 26] Empirical knowledge is confined to given facts, it can determine descriptively what the content of values is and what the possibility of realisation of these values is, but not whether one system or another should be chosen, nor whether the ends prescribed by certain values should be followed or not. The choice between values is a matter of *faith*: 'Only on the assumption of belief in the validity of values is the attempt to expouse value-judgements meaningful. However, to *judge* the validity of such values is a matter of *faith*'. [*Methodology* p. 55 (emphasis in the original)]

Science is provided with the objects it studies by 'cultural interests'; there is no empirical means of choice between these objects and no concepts by means of which they may be evaluated in respect of their *scientific* significance. At the most empirical knowledge can establish what the objective content of a value system is. Such an analysis is descriptive and can only lead to an 'understanding' of what such values and interests mean and, because it is purely descriptive, such analysis cannot lead to a scientific critique of the suitability of these values as means of provision of the objects of knowledge. Criticism is limited to investigating the coherence and the consequences of such value systems:

But the scientific treatment of value-judgements may not only understand and emphatically analyse (*nacherleben*) the desired ends and the ideals which underly them; it can also 'judge' them critically. This criticism can of course have only a dialectical character: i.e. it can be no more than a formal logical judgement of historically given value-judgements and ideas, a testing of the ideals according to the postulate of the internal *consistency* of the desired end. [*Methodology* p. 54 (emphasis in the original)]

Where the ends of a value system are clearly stated and consistent knowledge is silent; it cannot criticise, it can merely 'understand'.

The objects of cultural scientific knowledge are therefore given facts selected and ordered according to their significance relative to certain values. The unity of these facts as the object of a knowledge does not inhere in them but stems from the value categories in terms of which they are selected. Within the limits established by the 'transcendental presupposition' Weber retains the positivist position that the object of any science is a field of phenomena given to observation and which is designated as a unity analytically. The unity of particular objects of knowledge in the cultural sciences is a nominal one and it rests on non-empirical 'cognitive interests':

> The quality of an event as a 'social-economic' event is not something which it possesses 'objectively'. It is rather conditioned by the orientation of our cognitive interest, as it arises from the specific cultural significance which we attribute to the particular event in a given case. [*Methodology* p. 64]

Thus Weber defines the object of 'social-economics' as those phenomena that are analytically isolable as being concerned with the scarcity of means. This object is significant because it arises from the conflict of human subjects seeking to realise ends; social relations being conceived as purposive inter-subjectivity.

The Weberian object of knowledge has a dual character: it consists of phenomena given to experience ('facts') which are constituted as the coherent object of knowledge by values. 'Real' phenomena are isolated analytically as the object of a specific knowledge; the means of isolation of those phenomena from the 'infinite multiplicity' is their relevance to certain cultural values. *Values* define the analytically separate unity of the phenomena to be studied. The object of knowledge is *doubly given* to it: it is given by extra-scientific value systems and it is given as a realm of existent facts. Knowledge is constrained by values which are supposed to exist prior to it and which determine its content, and by a given field of phenomena it cannot question or alter. Hence the pertinence of the category of 'neo-Kantian positivism' with respect to Weber's epistemology; in that epistemology the neo-Kantian division of the objects of knowledge and the methodological rules of positivism are combined. Weber's position differs from classical positivism in that the unity of the object of knowledge is not derived from regularities observed in the phenomena or from analytic categories but from their significance for certain cultural values.

Objective knowledge is limited to a knowledge of values (necessarily descriptive) and to propositions about phenomena (selected by values). The methodological rules for the study of the given phenomena (nominalism, the separation of factual and evaluative propositions, the determining of the validity or empirical propositions by correspondence with the real) are the rules of positivism. Within the area defined by value-relatedness the positivist method holds sway, outside of the limits of the 'empirical' value-choices are the only means of deciding between one cultural scientific system and another.

Knowledge in the cultural sciences does not form a unified body of related propositions, laws and theories. The cultural sciences seek as the end of knowledge the comprehension of the concrete in all its individuality and uniqueness. The formation of general laws is not the objective of the cultural sciences. Analysis in terms of cultural significance is 'entirely different from the analysis of reality in terms of laws and general concepts'. [*Methodology* p. 77] Laws and general categories are merely a *means* to concrete knowledge: 'In the cultural sciences, the knowledge of the universal or general is never valuable in itself'. [*Methodology* p. 80] Laws and general concepts have at best an *heuristic* value. The positivist conception of laws, concepts and theories as constructions placed upon the phenomena, nominal, provisional and subject to refutation, nevertheless supposes that the aim of scientific knowledge is rigorous generalisation and that there are definite objective criteria of selection between and proof of concepts and theories. Generalisation is not the explanatory aim of Weberian knowledge and its concepts are not subject to definite objective criteria of proof. Indeed, there are no criteria of proof conceptual, empirical or otherwise for general concepts in Weber's epistemology. Concepts and categories are selected and rejected by the ambiguous test of their 'usefulness' as devices for reaching and illuminating the significance of the concrete.

Knowledge in the cultural sciences could not aspire to unity – its diversity is presupposed in the method by which its objects are constituted. Weber's rejection of Rickert's position on the existence of universal values tends to lead to a thoroughgoing relativism. There are potentially as many cultural scientific systems as there are systems of values; cultural significance is entirely relative to a particular value system. The cultural sciences necessarily generate a plurality of competing objects of knowledge: 'There is no absolutely "objective" scientific analysis of culture – or . . . of "social phenomena" independent of special and "one-sided" viewpoints according to which . . . they are selected, analysed and organised for expository purposes.' [*Methodology* p. 72] The relative significance of these different value systems is an evaluative question as is the question of the significance of the very category of culture itself:

> We have designated as 'cultural sciences' those disciplines which analyse the phenomena of life in terms of their cultural significance. The *significance* of a configuration of cultural phenomena and the basis of this significance cannot be derived and rendered intelligible by a system of analytic laws . . . since the significance of cultural events presupposes a *value-orientation* towards those events. The concept of culture is a *value concept*. [*Methodology* p. 74 (emphasis in the original)]

The generality of a value system is no proof of its validity: significance is entirely dependent on particular systems of values *as values*, and it does not depend on how popular or unpopular these values are. The choice of values, the means of defining the object of knowledge in the cultural sciences, is a matter of *faith* (belief in the validity of the values) or it is arbitrary and conventional (*some* perspective must be chosen) or it reflects an ulterior motive (a certain 'one-sided viewpoint' is chosen because it is useful for certain purposes of the knower).

'Culture' is defined by Weber's discourse as a privileged object of knowledge distinct from nature and the natural sciences, which is supposedly prior to all epistemological concepts or methodological rules. Weber maintains that 'the concept of culture is a value concept'. As such it cannot for him be subjected to epistemological criticism. A methodology based on empirical validation enters once the general object of knowledge 'culture' has been created by a value-choice common to all cultural scientific systems and the specific objects of investigation of particular cultural scientific knowledges are designated by particular value systems. Weber thus retains the empiricist conception of the object of knowledge as a given object at the same time as subjectivising and relativising the process by which that object is constituted for knowledge.

'Significance' is culturally relative, yet the empirical results which follow from the different and relative conceptions of the object of the cultural sciences are supposed to be as true as the empirical results of the natural sciences. 'Proven' hypotheses derived from value-related categories are true, however distinct the forms of cultural values from which the hypothetical propositions derive. The givenness of the 'facts' of the cultural realm means that, at the level of specific hypotheses, relativism is avoided. Specific hypotheses are to be set before the tribunal of the facts, as they are in classical positivism. Knowledge is unified at the level of the common validity of specific proven propositions about concrete cases, not in general laws or theories or through reference to universal values (Rickert). Knowledge is unified in that all these propositions are *true*, however diverse the historical individuals about which they are true or the categories from which the propositions derive. The facts, being given prior to knowledge, are equivalent. Weber is both a cultural relativist and a positivist. Relativism exists at the level of values and uniformity at the level of empirical propositions. The category 'neo-Kantian positivism' renders the specificity of Weber's thoroughgoing relativism and his commitment to proven 'empirical' knowledge.

This unity of relativism and 'empirical' knowledge is made possible through Weber's category of the 'ideal-type'. The ideal-type is the principal methodological means of establishing the cultural significance of phenomena and of deriving empirical propositions about them. The type is a 'one-sided accentuation' of reality; that is, the selection and formation of certain characteristics into a type according to definite 'cultural interests'. The type is a form of abstraction from cultural reality which through its one-sidedness selects and emphasises the cultural significance of a range of phenomena. This type is applied to the real in the form of a negative model, in which difference from as well as correspondence to the model can be measured in terms of its cultural significance. Thus, as we shall see, models of rational action provide the means of

determining the place of the irrational in specific events – the degree
of irrationality being measured by the deviation of the actual course
of action from the rational course. The type is therefore a means of
selection of the facts and a mechanism for specifying their significance.

'Ideal-typical' constructs are as relative as the systems of values
from which they are derived. Types are formed with reference to
objectives defined by values and the principles of selection which
govern the combination of elements in a type are determined by
the value system in question. Thus Weber argues: 'Inasmuch as
the "points of view" from which they can become significant for us
are very diverse, the most varied criteria can be applied to the
selection of the traits which are to enter into the construction of
an ideal-typical view of a particular culture.' [*Methodology* p. 91]
This produces a total relativisation of 'theory' in the cultural
sciences. Ideal-types are not *theories*, in the sense of general explanatory systems accounting for objects designated by the concepts of
these systems. Ideal-types are not generalisations derived from a
given range of 'facts' and subject to the proof of correspondence
with the 'facts'. Ideal-types are neither proven nor disproven: the
ideal-type 'is no "hypothesis" but it offers guidance to the construction of hypotheses.' [*Methodology* p. 90] Hypotheses derived from
an ideal-typical construction if proven or disproven do not prove
or disprove the type. In the first place the mode of derivation of
hypotheses from a type is not like the derivation of empirical propositions as deductions from theoretical statements. In the second
place the *deviation* of concrete conditions from the ideal-typical
model is one of the ways in which ideal-typical analysis operates.
There is no rigorous relation between ideal-types and the hypotheses
derived from them. 'Usefulness' in research is the sole criterion of
validation of ideal-types and this criterion is entirely evaluative and
cultural – it depends on the 'interests' of the knower whether an ideal
type is deemed 'useful' or not. Only specific empirical propositions
are subject to any kind of proof at all. Any value system can, at
least potentially, create the object of a cultural science. Ideal-types
derived from this value system if they are declared to be 'useful',
if they are logically consistent and not reducible to simpler types,
and if they are capable of bearing 'subjective meaning' are subject
to no proofs whatsoever. Weber justifies this purely heuristic status
of theory in the cultural sciences with a reference to neo-Kantian
epistemology:

If one perceives the implications of the fundamental ideas of modern epistemology which ultimately derives from Kant; namely, that concepts are primarily analytical instruments for the mastery of empirical data and can be only that, the fact that precise genetic concepts are necessarily ideal types will not come to cause him to desist from constructing them. [*Methodology* p. 106]

We will now turn from critical summary to criticism proper. The cultural sciences are concerned with the 'understanding' of value systems and with assessing the relationships between the ends derived from such systems and the means to their empirical realisa- tion. Explanation of values is not possible – values are ever pre- given to the cultural sciences. This supposed givenness of values to empirical knowledge has two sources in Weber's epistemology. The first source is that the very notion of 'culture' is itself taken to be a value; it is a 'transcendental presupposition' prior to all the concepts and empirical analyses of the cultural sciences. The existence of a realm of autonomous values cannot be subject to any form of criticism in the cultural sciences; 'culture' is the object pre-given to these sciences, pre-selected by an unquestionable value choice. If values were explicable in terms of causes or conditions of existence then this autonomous realm would cease to exist. The second source is that the valuing human subject is the content of this 'transcendental presupposition': culture consists in the freedom of the human subject to project meanings on to the world and to choose ends for its actions. The human subject as a free being endowing the world with meaning is presupposed as the fundamental element of Weber's cultural sciences. Weber gives primacy to what he calls the 'transcendental presupposition' of human freedom. End-realising behaviour is not caused but freely chosen by the subject. The essence of human freedom is the capacity of the subject to choose ends for itself. Choice, because it is free, cannot be subject to scientific analysis; if the choice of ends were explicable and determinable then human freedom would be limited. Weber's insistence on the separation of facts and values is thus conditioned primarily by the freedom of the subject to choose values indepen- dently of facts. The positivistic position on 'objectivity' is logically secondary to this. Subjectivism and positivism establish parallel and mutually reinforcing separations of fact and value in Weber's work. The division of knowledge into the establishment of value-related·

ness and specific empirical study which characterises Weber's epistemology derives from the means–ends schema of subjectively meaningful action. The supposition of the fundamental freedom of the human subject necessitates that values remain beyond knowledge. Paradoxically, this supposition of the freedom of the subject also creates the necessity of an objective and empirical analysis of means. Values are part of the realm of *ideas* and, therefore, of a realm of freedom. Ideas are not limited to the realisable; all that can be conceived is not all that is possible. Since values are *freely* chosen they are necessarily not chosen on the basis of an analysis of their realisability, such an analysis would limit human freedom and the ends possible to man. The transcendental and the quixotic would be banished once and for all. Culture is a realm of freedom. Action is a realm subject to limits. The means to the realisation of ends are objectively limited by the fact that action takes place in the world and demands material means; the ends of culture are realised in a world at least partly outside of culture. The freely chosen values of culture require an alien element for their realisation. Nature is a realm of objective limits beyond culture, the material means to human ends are not automatically given by this meaningless objectivity. The nature/culture distinction is not merely part of the overture to the cultural sciences, but plays a role in their positive content. It helps to explain why man's freedom in respect of values is not accompanied by man's freedom in the world. Scarcity, which has its origin in the niggardliness of nature, imposes limits on the ends realisable. The means to the realisation of ends are also limited by the fact that the freedom of choice of the subject in the realm of values necessitates the conflict between the ends of a plurality of subjects. Freedom in choice means that the ends chosen cannot necessarily be the same, indeed, the *difference* of values and ends is an index of freedom. Scarcity and human struggle create the problem of means. Not all ends are empirically realisable, certain means are inappropriate to certain ends, the ends of men are incompatible, therefore the means–ends relation is not given. The consequences of action cannot therefore be deduced from the ends of that action.

Weber's whole epistemological/sociological discourse is pivoted around what he calls a 'transcendental presupposition'. Essential elements of Weber's substantive sociology require the content of this 'presupposition', that is, the freedom of the human subject and the separation of values and facts which follows from it.

Weber conceives the freedom of the human subject as a *presupposition*, as prior to knowledge. It is essential to make a distinction here, between what Weber's discourse signifies and the means by which that signification is constituted. Weber presents us with a epistemology in which the nature and content of knowledge is determined, evaluatively and arbitrarily, prior to knowledge. But we must not assume that what Weber *says* he himself *does*. Weber *presupposes nothing*, his discourse tells us about presuppositions. The 'transcendental presupposition' is a concept or category in Weber's discourse, it is constituted discursively not presupposed.

Weber must consider human freedom to be a presupposition prior to knowledge, and not as a product of discourse, as a function of the means of knowledge. If he were not to do so then human freedom would be a *concept*, subject to disputation and proof, and not an unquestionable and essential precondition of knowledge. Let us be clear, we are not criticising Weber for presupposing, for going outside of discourse (that is impossible), rather we are criticising his giving the concept of presupposition a key place in his discourse. The effect of this designation of the unquestionable priority of human freedom *by* discourse is to limit the explanatory power of discourse, to close and to silence areas of problems and avenues of theorisation. This 'presupposition' introduces arbitrariness into discourse, certain objects and issues cannot be theorised or questioned since they are taken discursively to be presumed.

Weber's epistemology excludes any explanatory general theorisation from the cultural sciences. Weber's discussion of all epistemological problems in terms of the fact-value couple (which as we have seen is derived from the supposition of human free will) necessarily excludes the problem of theory, which consists neither in values nor in given facts. The elements of knowledge in the cultural sciences are, the knowing subject, 'values', and a facticity, composed of an infinite series of unique facts. Knowledge consists in value-related 'points of view' and specific empirical propositions. The object of the cultural sciences in general, 'culture', is conceived as presupposed prior to the operations of knowledge. The objects and problems of specific cultural scientific investigations, deriving from particular value systems, are likewise conceived as presupposed prior to the operations of 'empirical' knowledge. The objects and problems of the cultural sciences are constituted in such a way that theoretical criticism of the pertinence and rigour of these objects and problems is impossible. The space for theory is abolished from the cultural sciences: values are not theory and cannot be questioned by it, 'empirical' knowledge is an a-theoretical set of particular propositions. Weber uses the fact-value distinction as a means to exclude rigorous, general explanatory knowledge. The separation of value and fact, in its Weberian form, guarantees freedom of evaluative 'points of view' and freedom from theory.

The cultural scientific investigator is thereby given an absolute freedom in designating the object of investigation and the purpose of studying that object. This freedom of the knower from the limits of a definite theoretical scheme and definite modes of proof reflects the freedom of the realm of values. Why a certain value-standpoint is chosen, why certain problems are chosen for investigation, what the purposes of the investigation are, these are not 'scientific' (i.e. empirical) questions. 'Science' begins when the object and purposes of knowledge are already given. Knowledge is reduced to what specific human subjects choose to study. This knowledge can only be challenged evaluatively, its significance being questioned from another value-standpoint, or, it can be challenged at the level of the correspondence of specific hypotheses with the 'facts'.

The definition of the object of knowledge by values defines and circumscribes the whole process of knowledge. What 'facts' are to be studied (given that we accept for purposes of exposition Weber's notion of a given set of discrete 'facts') and the significance of the results of such study are determined evaluatively. Since Weber provides an even less rigorous account of the criteria by which the correspondence of 'hypotheses' with the 'facts' is to be judged than does positivism, we have no idea of how empirical (technical) knowledge operates. 'Hypotheses' are framed in such a way that empirical knowledge cannot question and the significance of the results of the operation of this knowledge is assessed independently of them. As we have seen, there is no necessary relation between 'hypotheses' and the categories from which they are derived. The content and status of all knowledge, even specific 'empirical' propositions, is determined by values. Values are beyond theoretical or empirical question.

Value systems are equivalent and incommensurable. Value-related studies cannot therefore be true or false, only more or less 'significant'. The result is that significance can only be decided socially; it will be judged relative to the dominant value system. Weber's position is that such judgements are evaluative, not epistemological;

they do not make the preferred value-related position superior. Weber's position is relativist and irrationalist. Relativism means that values are equivalent but that the value dominant in a given case prevails. Irrationalism that the choice of values is subject to no limits and that the dominance of certain values is in essence inexplicable (it has to be, otherwise it would limit the freedom of the subject – there is no sociological reduction/explanation of values in Weber, unlike certain other relativists like Mannheim). Knowledge is relativised and irrationalised in the interests of the freedom of the subject. The positivist and the rationalist ideal of objective knowledge is abandoned, Weber's 'positivism' exists only at the level of technique. Georg Lukács, a much maligned but most perceptive critic of Weber, recognised this restriction of objective knowledge to the level of technique to be at once a demand for objectivity (at the level of technique) and an embracing of irrationalism in every other respect:

> For him [Weber] only technical criteria can be expected from sociology; in other words, only 'which means appropirate for the achievement of a proposed end are appropriate or inappropriate' . . . , can be investigated . . . *Everything* else will be outside the domain of science, an 'irrational' article of faith. Thus, Weber demands the neutrality of sociology, the total absence of all value judgements, he desires it purged of all apparently irrational elements. However, this leads . . . to the irrationalisation of the development of the social totality. Here, in effect, the result is the affirmation that the irrational character of the 'choice of values' is profoundly rooted in social reality, without the realisation that this suppresses all rational method. [Lukács (1972) pp. 394–5]

Lukács recognises that Weber personally opposed the worship of irrationalism by such contemporaries as Stefan George and his circle, and also, that the structure of Weberian theory nevertheless leads to irrationalism.

Lukács also recognises the connection of Weberian epistemology with a definite conception of social relations, although he does so in a sociologistic and reductionist manner. The presupposition of human freedom links knowledge and social relations. The knower is necessarily given the same attributes as the human subjects he is to know. Objective knowledge, the objects and categories of which

are not reducible to the choice or purposes of any subject, knowledge based upon theoretical generality and non-subjective conditions of proof, cannot exist in the cultural sciences – it contradicts
the mysteries of human freedom. Like the social actor the cultural
scientist is free to choose the ends he will pursue and constrained by
objectivity only in the matter of means (and this constraint is
limited since technical knowledge is at the mercy of values). *Weber's
epistemological and sociological categories reflect their common
dependence on the conception of the free human subject.*

Knowledge and social action are both forms in which human
subjects choose ends and seek to realise them with appropriate
means. The categories of *Zweckrational* action and of empirical
knowledge in the cultural sciences are homologous. In both types
the end to be followed is a given and rationality or objectivity
consists in determining the most efficient means to the realisation
of that end or in applying means of knowledge to the study of the
realisation of ends. Rationality is concerned with the calculation of
appropriate means, scientific knowledge with the investigation of
the means–ends relationship. In both cases the ends of action and
of knowledge cannot be explained or questioned, rationality and
empirical knowledge are blind technique. The empirical scientist
and the bureaucrat are identical actors, instrumentalities to the
realisation of given ends.

Weber's reduction of science to value choices and to technique
is connected in his discourse with a definite conception of social
action. In knowledge and action the specific form in which human
freedom is presupposed leads to irrationalism and a cult of personal
freedom to choose. The cultural scientist and the social actor are
free to choose the 'values' which will guide their activities. 'Values'
are chosen by the subject alone and the process of choice and the
content of values is necessarily irrational (without calculation of
means).[1] This is the real sphere of human freedom. Technique is
a sphere of objective limitation of freedom, of the rule of instrumentality not of choice. At the *logical* level, therefore, there is a connection between Weber's epistemology and his conception of action; a
connection which finds its basis in the 'transcendental presupposition'
of human freedom.

Weber's fundamental typology of the forms of social action
(*Economy and Society* – hereafter *E&S* – vol. I, ch. 1) is a derivation from his conception of the human subject, i.e. man as a being
of purpose and a free agent in the matter of value-choice. The

c

attributes and possibilities of orientation of this subject appear in the content of the types. The differences between the types consist in the *nature* of the end towards which action is directed, the *source* of that end, and the character of the *means–ends relationship*. Because culture is a realm of freedom not all the ends conceivable in it are equivalent or empirically realisable. Ends may thus be divided into empirically realisable ends which are specific in content (the ends of *Zweckrational* action) and the ends of value systems which prescribe forms of conduct irrespective of the conditions of action (*Wertrational* action). Ends do not derive solely from values. Teleological action is not the exclusive form of human conduct. Action may arise from emotional states (*Affektual* action) or become atrophied into habit, the value-based purpose of action being lost in its ritualised perpetrations (*Traditional* action). These latter two forms of action are on the ' "borderline" of meaningfully oriented action'. [*E&S*, vol. I, p. 25] (Emotion and tradition can be made the objects of values, 'spontaneous' action or the 'traditional way' can be valued in themselves. Weber recognises this but places these forms of action on the 'borderline' because they do not correspond to teleological action in the strict sense.) In them action does not stem from values towards an end. Such action almost goes beyond the limit of meaningful action – the human subject choosing values and projecting meanings towards the world. In *Zweckrational* action the most efficient means to the realisation of the end are calculated, in *Affektual* action certain actions follow from emotional states irrespective of calculation, as they do from habit in *Traditional* action, and in *Wertrational* action action becomes conduct to be followed as an end in itself. *Zweckrational* and *Wertrational* action are the basic forms of 'meaningfully oriented action'. Both represent a simple extension of the notion of the human subject as a being of freedom and purpose which is supposed in Weber's epistemology. Social life could not be conceived otherwise than through the dominance of these types of action without contradicting the premises of cultural-scientific knowledge. Later we shall see that the *Zweckrational* action type dominates explanation in Weber's sociology.

We noted earlier that Weber's epistemology leaves no space for theory. Theory is replaced in the cultural sciences by typification. The type represents an 'accentuation' of the characteristics of cultural values, patterns of action, events, etc., into an abstract 'ideal' form – 'accentuation' is a process of selection according to a certain value-standpoint. Typification necessarily abandons the problem of *explanation* of social relations since it is supposed to be nothing more than a distillation of the elements existent in certain given cultural and historical forms.[2] The ideal-type selects and accentuates according to values. It is a value-motivated *re-presentation* of certain segments of cultural reality. In re-presenting and distilling the selected given forms nothing can be explained, only clarified. Further, there are as many distinct types as there are value-motivations for selection. Types may be logically clarified and classified under more general typifications, but they cannot be related one to another in any systematic and progressive way, unlike the relations of concepts in theoretical discourse.

Lukács is correct to designate typification as *formalism*. The ideal-type formalises the given and is then reapplied to it. Ideal-typical analysis is a variant of the epistemology of 'models'. It combines formalism, pragmatism and irrationality. Formalism is circular: reality is 'abstracted' into a model and the model reapplied to the real. Models are at best, on their own epistemological claims, a means of saving the phenomena. The criteria of abstraction, how models are formed, and of the 'fit' of the model with 'reality' are pragmatic, subject to no conditions of proof. The epistemology of models leads directly to *conventionalism*; those models which save the phenomena best are to be preferred and, where models have equal capacities in this respect subsidiary criteria of economy, elegance, etc., must be introduced. In Weber's case pragmatism is further reinforced by the use of models in a negative mode, in which deviations from the model demonstrate the causal role of forms other than those of the model (this deviation, needless to say, cannot be subjected to rigorous measurement). Irrationality, as we have seen above, enters into ideal-typical analysis in that the selection of elements to form the type and the problems to which the type is applied are both determined by unquestionable value-motivations. In the selection inevitable in the two movements of accentuation and application which complete the circle of formalism the whole process of typification is entirely subject to the 'motives' of the knowing subject. In this respect ideal-typical analysis is inferior to the positivist forms of the epistemology of models.

Typification is, as Lukács argues, 'the primary task of sociology' [1972, p. 393], since sociology is concerned with the typical and general and history with the concrete and individual. Sociology (as conceived in *Economy and Society*) constructs types of recurrent cultural forms and patterns of action. Its primary function, apart from accounting for typical and recurrent behaviour, is to provide conceptual types for the historian. Sociology is primarily a form of provision of methodological means to the empirical sociologist and the historian. Ultimately the general sociologists' types are of value if they are 'useful' to the empirical sociologist and historian. Here, formalism itself becomes technique and the sociologist the technician. Values are used to produce formalised ideal-typical descriptions; they are means for historical research, neither proven nor disproven, instrument which are more or less useful. It is the historian who embodies the purposes of genuine cultural scientific knowledge, who selects from the types available according to his value-related problem. Yet these formal/instrumental types are not free from relation to values, to select and construct the general sociologist must *adopt* values. If they are not his own or do not represent purposes of his own, then the sociologist is like an epistemological ventriloquist's dummy who adopts or takes up values to provide a battery of ideal-typical instruments for the historian. His relation to knowledge is doubly technical; he is an instrument of historical knowledge and his relation to values is an instrumental consequence of that instrumentality. *Economy and Society* explicitly adopts this position: 'Its method . . . makes no claim to any kind of novelty. On the contrary it attempts only to formulate what empirical sociology really means when it deals with the same problems . . .' [vol. I, p. 3] This insistence on sociology as technique doubly displaces values and doubly reinforces the dominance of their irrationality. Values are displaced into the empirical sociologist or historian as the genuine knowing subject, and displaced on to instrumentality; values are 'adopted' for methodological purposes. Values are dominant in knowledge nevertheless. The historian, etc., selects from these types with his own value motives in mind. However instrumentally the sociologist's adoption of values is conceived, his choice is doubly arbitrary: the value-motivated types constructed still embody values not subject to question or proof, and behind instrumentality there must be some definite basis of selection. Thus while 'sociology parades as a science auxiliary to history' [Lukács (1972) p. 392] this *parade* does not legitimate or give a rational form to the methodology of ideal-types.

4

The Theory of Social Action

There is no serious contradiction between the epistemology of the 'cultural sciences' advanced in the methodological essays and the conception of sociological knowledge advanced in *Economy and Society*. Weber's sociological categories entail and produce the content of the very same transcendental 'presupposition'. That is, the human subject as a being free to project meanings and to seek ends is at the basis of Weber's general sociology. It is from the attributes of this free human subject that the nature of the object of sociology is derived.

Weber defines the object of sociology thus: 'Sociology . . . is a science concerning itself with the interpretative understanding of social action and thereby with a causal explanation of its course and consequences.' [*E&S*, vol. I, p. 4]

The nature of *social* action is derived from the relation of the subject to its own meanings and intentions. The subject's relations to its own actions provide the means of defining what sociology is: 'action' exists 'when and in so far as the acting individual attaches a subjective meaning to behaviour'; *social action* exists when the meaning of the subject 'takes account of [the] behaviour of others' and is other-oriented in form. [*E&S*, vol. I, p. 4] Social action thus depends on the individual subject's subjective representation of and relation to his own behaviour, if it is conscious, 'meaningful' and other-regarding it is social.

It should be noted before we continue that Weber never defines the content of the term 'subjective meaning'. Subjective meaning is pre-social or not necessarily social; it precedes the definition of social action in the logic of the discourse and helps to establish it. Meaning in this sense cannot be the product of language or other significatory system, for it would then be already social or other-regarding. Any language, whether it is a private invention or not, necessarily includes *discourse* as a condition of signification, and discourse involves the *place* of the other, although not necessarily two concrete subjects. Discourse is inherently other-regarding. Weber's subjective meaning must therefore be significance or value for a pure consciousness. It is pre-social and pre-linguistic, a property of consciousness. Weber's subject is the pure subject of classical philosophy – a pure pre-social consciousness.

Meaning, and therefore action, only exists through human purpose:

> . . . process or conditions, whether they are animate or inanimate, human or non-human, are . . . devoid of meaning in so far as they cannot be related to an intended purpose. That is to say, *they are devoid of meaning if they cannot be related to action in the role of means or ends*, but constitute only the stimulus, the favouring or hindering circumstances. [*E&S*, vol. I, p. 7]

Action is not possible without purpose; in the absence of intention there is mere caused behaviour. No meaning can be attached to non-teleological behaviour. The essence of meaning is that it is projected on to the world, that it gives rise to subjective ends and exists as the adoption and pursuit of ends. Without purpose and intention, meaning and values cannot exist. 'Values' presuppose intentions and therefore ends – to value something in preference to something else is to stand in a definite relation to them as ends or means of action. Man is a being capable of meaningful action because he is free to will, to choose between directions for his behaviour.

Sociology is a cultural and not a natural science. It deals with purposive action rather than caused behaviour. Culture is a realm of freedom because it is based on subjective will. Behaviour that derives from circumstances and is not chosen is extra-social and extra-human. Sociology finds its point of departure in and its categories are subordinate to the attributes of the human subject – free will and meaning.

Meaning is the attribute of two categories of subject in Weber's sociology:

(i) The actual meanings of concrete existent human subjects;
(ii) The meaning of abstract (hypothetical) ideal-typical subjects. Such subjects are conceptual constructions of possible actors and to posit the meaning of such an actor involves the construction of a *typical form of action*.

Sociological categories select and order empirical sociological observations of concrete courses of action into consistent general types. The construction of such typical forms of action is the basic task of sociology, this is because all social relations are ultimately nothing more than forms of action of individual human subjects. In sociology, therefore, subjects of type (ii) will necessarily take precedence over subjects of type (i).

Ideal-typical categories of action take the form of the construction of a relation of the actor to other subjects and to the word (meaning-purpose) and the mode in which that relation can be actualised in behaviour (means–ends relation). Action is meaningful, social and explicable in so far as it embodies purpose; ideal types of *social* action must therefore have a purpose or intention inscribed in them. Explanation of action requires that certain ideal-typical forms predominate:

> *For the purposes of typological scientific analysis it is convenient to treat all irrational, affectually determined elements of behaviour as factors of deviation from a conceptually pure type of rational action . . . Only in this way is it possible to assess the causal significance of irrational factors as accounting for deviations from this type.* [*E&S*, vol. I, p. 6 (my emphasis)]

The passage quoted is a most significant one and it requires an extended commentary to bring out all of its implications. It reveals the essence of Weber's sociology. Its subjectivism combined with the subordination of the meanings of concrete subjects to 'typical' forms embodied by abstract subjects. Its commitment to teleological causality which promotes one abstract type of action, *Zweckrational* action, to theoretical dominance. The implications of this passage are as follows.

(i) Sociology is the interpretative and *therefore* causal explanation of social action. Explanation is interpretative-causal because it is on the basis of understanding the meanings of the actor that the purpose of his action can be known; only then is it possible to chart the fate of the realisation of that purpose in terms of the available means and the purposes of other subjects. Causal analysis is analysis of the relation between ends and their outcomes. Social life is teleological; it consists of end-realising action by human subjects. Social relations are the products of the intersecting teleologies of interacting subjects and the outcomes which result from these projects. Causal analysis must be analysis of the realisation of purpose and not of the non-purposive determination of behaviour.

(ii) The understanding of action operates through ideal-typical constructions of action. 'Rational' action is the fundamental form of teleological (and therefore of meaningful) action, it is the positing of a definite end by the subject and the conscious deployment of means to its realisation. Action which does not take this form is 'irrational', that is, not properly teleological. By means of the rational form of teleology the irrational factors affecting human wills and projects become calculable as deviations from the course rational action would have followed. *'Rationality' is methodologically the norm against which all human behaviour is to be measured.*

(iii) Weber's sociology starts from the category of social action. This is defined as the relation of the subject to his own acts (they are intentional and other-oriented), but this relation of the subject to his acts is separated from the subject in sociology's analysis of social behaviour. This separation takes place on two levels. The first level is that the means of understanding of the action of the concrete subject are not the meanings of the concrete subject itself but of a 'typical' subject constructed by and at the will of the observer. The second level is that 'rational' action is a negative model through which the causal effectivity of irrational action is *accounted for* rather than that the content or subjective meaning of that irrational action is *understood*. Social action is therefore defined not by the relation of the subject to his actions (as is claimed) but by the construction of the relation of an abstract subject to possible actions and this relation is one of 'rationality'.

Through the methodological norm of 'rationality' irrational action (and this clearly implies not simply 'affectual' action but all action without a clear representation of ends and a rationalised means–ends relation) is known by its *consequences and not by the determination of the subjective meaning of the actor*. Its causal effectivity is discovered by the degree of deviation from the objectively rational course, by the degree of absence of rationality. Hence the interpretative categories through which action is understood are always those of 'rational' action even when the subjective meaning dominant in the situation is an 'irrational' one. Not only is irrational action 'understood' through its inverse, but concrete 'rational' action is not known to be such through the subjective meanings of the actor but through the correspondence of its consequences with those predicted by an ideal-typical model. The

correspondence of rational action with the course and outcome pos-
tulated by the model is the sole form in which its 'rationality' can
be determined, 'rationality' being a general type and not a concrete
course of action. *Subjective* meaning is determined by its opposite,
the *situation* of action (that is, the extra-subjective form of an
action – its course and consequences), and by means of an ideal-
typical norm.

Weber makes this dominance of the norm of rationality most
explicit. Sociological laws

> are . . . typical probabilities confirmed by observation to the
> effect that under certain given conditions an expected course of
> .ction will occur, which is understandable in terms of the *typical*
> motives and *typical* subjective intentions of the actors. *These*
> *generalisations are both understandable and definite in the highest*
> *degree in so far as the typically observed course of action can be*
> *understood in terms of the purely rational pursuit of an end, or*
> *where for reasons of convenience such a theoretical type can be*
> *heuristically employed.* [*E&S*, vol. I, p. 18 (my emphasis)]

The reason for the imposition of this typical norm should now be
clear: Weber starts from a definite anthropological position that
the human subject is an evaluating and purposive being. Human
action that does not fall within the scope of this conception of the
subject must be of a subordinate or of a sub-human form. The
ontological assumption of human freedom inevitably involves an
ethics, a presumption and a prescription in favour of the forms of
action appropriate to freedom. In Weber's case this *ethics* (explicit
and rigorous in such thinkers as Rousseau and Kant) becomes a
methodology. The presumption of freedom and rationality as forms
within the real becomes the transformation of such forms into
'heuristic devices', into apparently neutral methods of knowledge.
The methodological dominance of 'rationality' is a function of the
fact that 'rationality' is nothing but effective *teleological* action.

Sociological knowledge attains certainty to the degree to which
the means–ends relationship in action corresponds to the pure
form of teleological action. Rational action is the means of calculation of all other forms of action since it permits the construction
of a precise model of means, ends and consequences. The concrete
existence of this pure type of rational action is very infrequent –
all action mixes rationality and irrationality in varying degrees.

D

However, this mixture can only be unravelled by means of the calculable nature of rational (teleological) action. Rationality is therefore the *model* against which all other forms of action and all concrete courses of action are measured.

The contrast with Rousseau is striking. The presumption of freedom as part of the human essence and the fact of unfreedom leads to an *ethical* norm, man should be free. Rousseau recognises the discrepancy: 'Man is born free and everywhere he is in chains.' Freedom must, if need be, be imposed as a norm. The Will-of-All is not equivalent to the General Will. The means to remove the reign of narrow self-interest and to force men to act in freedom according to their nature must be created by legislation and maintained by institutions. For Weber the fact that the essential form of meaningful social action is not necessarily the dominant form leads to a *methodological* norm; action is only intelligible in so far as it is known through the essential form of purposive social action.

This dominance of rational models of action involves all the limitations of Weber's ideal-type method. The relation of the type to the concrete is arbitrary and ambiguous, at the control of the 'observer'. How is the degree of deviation from the model measured? It is controlled by the content of the model and the calculation of 'fit' with the concrete by the 'observer'. The process of selection of the elements which form the model is entirely in the hands of the model-maker – thus Weber's conception of economic 'rationality' is nothing more than a certain form of capitalist calculation. The degree of 'deviation' of economic action from the model (if we accept for a moment that economies are forms of inter-subjective action) is entirely determined by the process of selection. Capitalist calculation corresponds to it and is 'rational'; other forms do not and are more or less irrational. The process of application of the type is subject to the calculations the 'observer' makes as to what it is to be applied to and of the degree of deviation he discovers. Even if one were to accept the epistemology of models it is clear that Weber's position allows an uncontrollable degree of freedom to the model-constructor/'observer' to embody his ideological 'interests' in models and read off the content of this ideology as results. Given this 'play' in the construction of models and their application, the *subjective meaning of the actor is in the hands of the interpreter of action*. Far from 'understanding' the meanings of concrete subjects Weber's ideal-type method gives significance to these meanings according to its own processes of selection and valuation. The concrete subject is present in Weber's sociology as the supposed object of understanding and absent in its actual operations of knowledge; this is because it is abstract 'typical' subjects embodying the purposes of the scientific subject which are the true object of knowledge. The knower, the scientific subject, enjoys an absolute freedom in respect of the concrete bestowed on him by Weber's epistemology and his sociological categories.

The conception of sociology as the interpretative–causal analysis of purposive other-regarding subjective action entails a thoroughgoing nominalism with respect to all categories of 'social structure'. Collectivities are nothing but the products of the action of individual subjects:

> for the subjective interpretation of action in sociological work these collectivities (States, corporations, etc.) must be treated as *solely* the resultants and modes of organisation of particular acts of individual persons, *since* these alone can be treated as agents in a course of subjectively understandable action. [*E&S*, vol. I, p. 13]

Teleological causality based on human wills must dissolve social relations into inter-subjective relations. For social relations to provide the conditions of existence of action would mean that an external supra-subjective cause determines subjective behaviour. Social institutions must, therefore, be considered solely as inter-subjective relations. Institutions are effective as inter-subjectivity in that one *subject* provides another with the conditions of his action in the form of ends, meanings, means, etc. Inasmuch as some subjects' behaviour is controlled from without, it is controlled not by impersonal forces but by other subjects. The sole form in which collectivities are real is when they are subjectively meaningful and provide the basis for human action with regard to that meaning: 'when reference is made in a sociological context to a state, a nation, a corporation, a family, or an army corps, or to similar collectivities, what is meant is, on the contrary, *only* a certain kind of development of actual or possible social actions of individual persons'. [*E&S*, vol. I, p. 14]

Thus subjectivism and positivist epistemology overlap and reinforce one another to entail the nominalisation of concepts of social structure and methodological individualist forms of explanation.

The dominant categories in terms of which Weber conceives

social relations are thus inter-subjective relations: legitimate domination, struggle and selection, etc. All these forms make possible a social world in which certain subjects are not free to entertain alternative ends, to project purposes, or to choose their means but in which their unfreedom stems from no non-teleological necessity, *but from the wills of other human subjects*. In domination one subject makes another's purpose the content of his own will, in selective struggles (such as the market) subjects compete to attain their ends. Domination and selection imply *superior* subjects. These superior subjects impose their will and ends upon others, they use them as *means* to their own ends. All processes of selection imply the dominance of characteristics: 'which are unusual, or . . . which are not possessed by the mediocre majority'. [*E&S*, vol. I, p. 39] All men are free but not all men are equal. Starting from the valuing and purposive subject, a being necessarily free in its choice of ends, Weber is led to account for oppressive and exploitative social relations as relations between human subjects, and not as impersonal systems of social relations. The *Übermensch* is present in the logic of Weber's sociology.

But no inter-subjective relation is final, inevitable, and beyond human control; domination presupposes the constant *act* of submission of the subject, selection and struggle never cease. Relations between men lack the certainty of relations between things. All Weber's concepts of relationships are therefore probabilistic. The concepts of power, class, etc., express *probabilities* of relations between subjects or conditions of subjects. Power depends on actually influencing others' actions, class on the struggles on the market. What power *is*, what class *is*, are empirical matters, decided by human struggles. Here again there is a correspondence between subjectivism and positivism: the freedom of the subject necessitates the statement of relations in a probabilistic form, a form of relation favoured in certain positivist epistemologies.

There is a necessary correspondence between Weber's conception of the object of sociology and ideal-typical analysis. Social relations are a product of inter-subjective action, action which is purposive. Explanation must therefore be in terms of human purposes and their consequences. It must be teleological, and 'rationality' is the pure form of teleology. The 'rational' action type reconstructs concrete social action in a form appropriate to the suppositions of the theory. 'Types' must be applied in a negative and displaced relation to the concrete, because the concrete has no necessary content. Social relations have no determinate nature or forms, since inter-subjective relations stem from human purposes freely chosen. Unlike Marxism, in which definite systems of social relations are supposed to have a necessary content and therefore theories of specific types of social totality, capitalism, socialism, etc., are possible, Weber's interpretative–causal sociology cannot permit a determinate relation between concepts and the concrete. Such a relation denies the dominance of values and the reign of freely chosen human purposes. '*Types*' are not *theories* but a means for a knowing subject to construct the world of purposive social action according to his own purposes. The insistence on the freedom of the subject as knower and as social actor prohibits rigorous and determinate social knowledge subject to definite conditions of proof. Irrationality and ambiguity are necessary to 'freedom'.

5

The Three Types of Legitimate Domination

Weber's two formulations of the three types of legitimate domination in *Economy and Society* are not an attempt to provide a rigorous general theory of the state, of its variant forms and of the conditions of political rule. Weber is quite explicit about this. His conception of these types is no different from the other categories of *Economy and Society*. They are abstract ideal-typical forms which may be of use to the empirical investigator. Weber's categories of political action are not a *theory*, a logical structure of concepts which designates an object to be explained and which provides a mechanism of explanation for that object, rather these categories are *tools* which the empirical investigator may find more or less useful: 'The usefulness of the above classifications can only be judged by its results in promoting systematic analysis'. [*E&S*, vol. I, p. 216] Weber's categories are not claimed to be general or exhaustive: 'The idea that the whole of concrete historical reality can be exhausted in the conceptual scheme about to be developed is as far from the author's thoughts as anything could be'. [ibid., loc. cit.] These categories are not systematic. The relation of the types is definitional and classificatory. They do not represent distinct forms of state, they are categories which can be used in various combinations in the analysis of specific political forms, nor do they form an historical sequence. How the types are used and combined is left to the empirical investigator.

If Weber is taken at his word these types cannot be criticised theoretically. They can only be found to be more or less useful by doing Weberian 'empirical' sociology. They cannot be criticised theoretically like a general theory because they are not one. Why, however, should Weber be taken at his word? These categories are proposed as means of analysis of politics and the state, and, if we accept them, as a substitute for other forms of analysis of politics and the state. Modern sociology has not taken Weber at his word either; Weber's categories are proposed as a substantive analysis of politics, an alternative to and a superior replacement for the outmoded and dogmatic concepts of Marxism. The pertinence of the questions asked in Weber's types about politics and the state can be questioned as can the theoretical conclusions to which they lead. Weberian epistemology attempts to put itself beyond criticism, or rather, limit criticism to its friends, the Weberian 'empirical' sociologists, who cannot help but find it 'useful'.

Weber's epistemology prevents him from giving any definite theoretical form to the social totality. His categories are formal and nominal, without definite theoretical relations one to another. However, areas of social life are differentiated by and for the purposes of categorical analysis. It is difficult to understand the place of Weber's category of domination in the system of types and its specific categorical content unless it is recognised that 'domination' is only made possible by the distinction between economic action and domination. 'Economic action is a *peaceful* use of the actors control over resources . . . to economic ends'. [*E&S*, vol. I, p. 63] The economic is 'concerned with the satisfaction of a desire for utilities'. [ibid., loc. cit.] Economic action concerns the peaceful use of resources to meet desired needs, as such it has no connection *as a category* with domination. Weber considers that 'factual power' which stems from control over resources is to be distinguished as a category from domination:

And yet, if we wish at all to obtain fruitful distinctions within the continuous stream of actual phenomena, we must not overlook the clear-cut antithesis between factual power which arises completely out of possession and by way of interest compromises in the market, and on the other hand, the authoritarian power of a patriarch or monarch with its appeal to the duty of obedience simply as such. [*E&S*, vol. III, p. 945]

Domination is limited to the mastership of man over man: 'in our terminology *domination* shall be identical with authoritarian *power of command*'. [*E&S*, vol. III, p. 946] The category of domination has no relation to the economy, it is defined quite separately from it.

The Weberian categories of 'economic action' and 'domination' do not define specific and articulated structures of social relations, they are not equivalents of the Marxist concepts of the 'economic structure' and the state. There is no necessary structure of social relations 'the economy' for Weber. Economic action is defined by the relation of the subject to his acts, the 'economy' is a formal relation of individual actions. Weber's conception of the economy is similar to that of Austrian marginalism, as we shall see. 'Domination' is a relation between human subjects that can exist in various forms, between a father and his sons, between a religious leader and his followers, etc. 'Domination' as an inter-subjective relation can exist wherever there are human subjects who give and obey commands; it is not a structure of social relations like the state.

The categories of 'economic action' and 'domination' are defined as separate and independent entities, hence there can be no *general* analysis of the relation of the economic and the political in Weber's system. The specific relations of economics and politics in concrete cases are empirically variable and no generalisations can be made from them. They are a matter of 'empirical' analysis and each case may be different. This is particularly clear in Weber's discussion of 'Status Groups and Classes' in vol. I of *Economy and Society*.

Weber's categories do not provide as many modern sociologists believe an alternative theorisation of the social totality to that of Marx, more 'empirical' and 'multi-factorial', *they abolish the notion of social totality as such*. Social relations disappear into inter-subjective relations. Weber's categories are applied to a concrete human milieu without any general or necessary structure. There is no social topography in Weber's conception, social relations are reduced to the plane of inter-subjective relations.

LEGITIMATE DOMINATION[1]

Domination is 'the probability that a command with a given specific content will be obeyed by a given group of persons'. [*E&S*, vol. I, p. 53] Domination is defined in inter-subjective terms – it is made possible by and exists in the obedience of one subject to another. The superior subject depends on the response of the subordinate for his will to become power. The primacy of the problem of legitimacy in Weber's categories of domination follows from the conception of domination as exclusively a relation between human subjects. The problem of legitimacy is central to such a conception since it concerns the conditions of existence of domination. Domination exists when subjects obey commands, hence it finds its conditions of existence in the reasons why subjects obey. Because human subjects are cultural beings and sociology is concerned with *action*, domination, to be social, must rest upon subjectively meaningful conditions of compliance and not external brute force which merely compels certain behaviours. Domination as pure force could not be part of sociology as an 'interpretative understanding of social action'. Legitimation is central because it provides subordinate subjects with subjectively meaningful reasons to obey by free act of will; it makes domination a social relationship: '. . . every genuine form of domination implies a minimum of voluntary compliance, that is, an interest (based on ulterior motives or genuine acceptance) in obedience'. [*E&S*, vol. I, p. 212]

Every form of domination entails a *dominant subject* (an individual or group of individuals who give orders), a *staff* which executes this subject's orders, and *subordinate subjects* who obey them. The relation of the staff to the dominant subject is the first defining characteristic of any form of domination: 'The members of the administrative staff may be bound to obedience to their superior (or superiors) by customs, by affectual ties, by a purely material complex of interests, or by ideal (*Wertrational*) motives. The quality of these motives largely determines the type of domination'. [*E&S*, vol. I, p. 213] In the first instance the type of domination depends on the motives for compliance of the staff. Where the basis of loyalty of the staff to their superiors consists in purely material interests 'a relatively unstable situation' results. Domination does not limit itself to material, ideal or affectual motives for compliance: 'In addition every such system attempts to establish and to cultivate a belief in its legitimacy. *But according to the kind of legitimacy which is claimed, the type of administrative staff developed to guarantee it, and the mode of exercising authority, will all differ fundamentally.*' [ibid., loc. cit. (author's emphasis)] Legitimacy exists when a form of domination is recognised as worthy of obedience as such, irrespective of other motives. Legitimacy is not merely a basis for compliance of the staff but of all subordinate subjects.

The mode of claiming legitimacy is the form in which types of domination are differentiated and classified: '. . . it is useful to classify the types of domination according to the kind of *claim* to legitimacy typically made by each'. [ibid., loc. cit. (author's emphasis)] Different types of domination are differences in the forms of *claiming* legitimacy, and if Weber's theory restricted itself to this level the analysis of types of domination would be nothing more than an account of justificatory ideologies. However, Weber argues that the type of claim to legitimacy is largely responsible for real differences in the organisation and the effectiveness of forms of rule. In the earlier version in Vol. III this is especially clear:

> For our limited purposes, we shall emphasize those basic types of domination which result when we search for the ultimate grounds of the *validity* of a domination . . . For a domination, this kind of justification of its legitimacy is much more than a matter of theoretical or philosophical speculation; it rather constitutes the basis of very real differences in the empirical structure of domination. [*E&S*, vol. III, p. 953]

The structure of domination derives from the mode in which legitimacy is claimed. The term *basis* is used to express this relation: the grounds for claiming legitimacy 'constitute the *basis* of' differences in the organisation of domination. Forms of rule are not derived from the material social conditions of existence which necessitate them, but, rather, they are seen as extensions of and derivations from the ideologies which legitimate them. For the purposes of categorical analysis forms of domination are derived from and defined as consequences of forms of legitimatory ideology.

The Weberian will interject that all this is entirely in the realm of the categorial and that no causality is implied in this primacy of legitimation. Weber, however, clearly asserts that legitimation constitutes the basis of differences in the *empirical*, this is not simply a choice of emphasis for heuristic purposes. Even if it were, the categories are defined in such a way that the structure of domination is derived from the mode of legitimation – this is the categorical content of the types and, given the *carte blanche* of the Weberian 'empirical' investigator, the effects of this categorical content will be registered in the nature and content of 'empirical' enquiries. There is no way that the Weberian can escape the idealist causality inscribed in the derivation of the types of domination from the *claims* to legitimacy. Legitimation must effect the form of rule in

Weber's conception. Command and obedience are the essence of rule, the existence and form of domination will therefore depend on how and why subjects obey commands.

The nature of a form of domination is defined by the mode in which it claims legitimacy, by the form in which subjectively meaningful reasons for compliance are created in the subordinate subjects. On the basis of these subjective meanings they obey commands voluntarily. Legitimacy is not guaranteed: 'Naturally, the legitimacy of a system of domination may be treated sociologically only as the *probability* that to a relevant degree the appropriate attitudes will exist, and the corresponding practical conduct ensue'. [*E&S*, vol. I, p. 214] Human subjects are free in the sense that their actions are *willed*, true compliance depends therefore on the grounds for legitimacy becoming the subjective meaning of the subordinates' action. If this is not the case then compliance is based on 'interest' or force and must be more or less unstable.

It would therefore seem essential for the Weberian analysis of domination to investigate the subjective conditions of compliance in any concrete case, for only the grounds of compliance can tell us how reliable is the obedience to commands of the subjects and how stable the form of domination. This, however, is not the case.

That subjects submit for reasons other than those imputed in the form of legitimation is of minor importance in the analysis of domination:

But these considerations are not decisive for the classification of types of domination. *What is important is the fact that in a given case the particular claim to legitimacy is to a significant degree and according to its type treated as 'valid'*; that this fact confirms the position of the persons claiming authority and that it helps to determine the choice of means of its exercise. [*E&S*, vol. I, p. 214]

Whatever the subjects' meanings or motives, the fact that they do *obey* and in the form of the domination's requirements of obedience confirms its legitimacy. So long as the claims to legitimacy are treated as 'valid', to a 'significant degree', that is, to the extent that these forms are not explicitly rejected, that men comply with the outward signs of obedience to legitimate authority, then rule is legitimated. Weber's doctrine may be taken as an inversion of Pascal's famous aphorism: enter the Church, kneel, mouth the

words of prayer, and you will *appear* to believe and that will satisfy
the Fathers. This position is also explicitly stated in the version
in Vol. III:

> The merely external fact of the order being obeyed is not suffi-
> cient to signify domination in our sense; we cannot overlook the
> meaning that the command is accepted as a 'valid' norm . . . In
> a concrete case the performance of the command may have been
> motivated by the ruled's own conviction as to its propriety, or
> by his sense of duty, or by fear, or by 'dull' custom, or by
> desire to obtain some benefit for himself. Sociologically, those
> differences are not necessarily relevant. [*E&S*, vol. III, p. 947]

The second part of this passage contradicts the first. In the first
the subjective meaning of the actor is of some consequence, in the
second it is not and the forms of meaning in which he acts are
primary. Commands are accepted as being 'valid' to the ruled unless
there are definite meanings or actions which indicate that they are
not. 'Sociologically' this means that if a command is obeyed it is
indeed taken to be accepted as valid. Acceptance is a proof of
validity.

'Genuine' domination has ceased to be a problem. Instead of
determining the meaning for the actor Weber derives the meaning
from the act. Within Weber's problematic it is logical that the fact
of obedience should in general be taken as indicating legitimacy,
however contradictory this might appear. Cynical interest or simple
coercion could not form a stable form of rule, since human action
depends upon will and men are free to obey or not. Stability supposes
either obedience through legitimacy or sub-social action through
habit and fear. The latter alternative does not really figure since it
would explain social forms by non-social behaviour. In spite of the
centrality of legitimacy to Weber's categories of domination, they
are not concerned with the fate of the ruled. In essence the primary
focus of interest is the quality of ruler and the type of political–
cultural life that forms of legitimation create. The derivation of the
form of rule from the *claim* to legitimation and not from the
commitment of the ruled is not accident. It is the quality of effect
generated by the *form* of legitimation which matters; here is what
Weber has to say about plebiscitary democracy: 'Regardless of
how its real value as an expression of the popular will may be
regarded, the plebiscite has been the specific means of deriving the

legitimacy of authority from the confidence of the ruled, even though the voluntary nature of such confidence is only formal or fictitious'. [*E&S*, vol. I, p. 267]

That the ruled vote and legitimate their leaders is sufficient, their specific relation to this act is of no consequence if it allows the rulers to claim legitimacy and to act as legitimate authority. Having voted, the people are of no account, the leaders can get on with their business.

The obedience of the subordinate which serves to define the problematic of domination is largely displaced as its questions and categories are developed. Given the existence of a form of domination, obedience to command in the forms that it specifies legitimates it; there is no need to explore the subjective meaning of obedience for the ruled. This derivation of the forms of rule from the *claim* to legitimacy is not only idealist, it is an apologia for oppression. This theory largely ignores the problem of why the masses obey if it is not through willing compliance. The theory has no formal need to pose it since the categories concern not real forms of state but the most general relationships of 'domination'. However, in practice these categories of domination are used as means of analysis of political life and of the state. Here the question is not formal and does matter. Weber's theory mystifies the conditions of 'domination' by so posing the problem that the apparatuses, instruments, and sources of state power are ignored or derived from its claim to legitimacy. Outside of Weber's categories it is clear that the masses 'obey' states not for the reasons claimed by legitimating ideologies but because of the concrete mechanisms of compliance which the state as a social institution possesses. The source of these state powers is not some legitimatory *claim* but the political relation of social and economic forces to the state. To examine the conditions of existence of the state in terms of its claims to legitimacy is to take the ideological form of the state at face value and to deduce from 'obedience' the effectivity of legitimation. When a large proportion of the world's population is subject to military dictatorships or other forms of authoritarian rule Weber's theory is not simply wrong and obfuscatory, it is an authoritarian political ideology.

Weber's categories in practice ignore the conditions of compliance of the subject and deduce the 'legitimacy' of the form of rule from its stable existence. Wolfgang Mommsen has recognised this fact most clearly:

Yet if we try to push the issue further in order to find substantive reasons why and under which conditions a system may be legitimate, we hit a vacuum . . . Legitimacy, in Weber's terms, amounts to little more than an equivalent of the stability of the respective political system. In other words there cannot be other than 'legitimate' systems of domination. [Mommsen (1974), p. 84]

Mommsen is less clear about the reasons why this is the case. Obviously, there cannot be other than 'legitimate' systems of domination. Illegitimate domination is an absurd category, Q.E.D. The reason why Weber's theory pays so little attention to the subjective conditions of compliance is more complex. It has to do *with what obedience means*, whether one enters into it entirely willingly or not. Weber's theory is not interested in the ruled not simply because Weber himself was not a democrat but because of what the ruled become when they submit to their rulers. This unconcern for the ruled is not an intrusion of Weber's personal political concerns into the theory but has a basis in the logic of the theory itself.

Weber defines obedience thus: 'Obedience will be taken to mean that the action of the person obeying follows in essentials such a course that the content of the command may be taken to have become the basis of action for its own sake'. [*E&S*, vol. I, p. 215] The version in Vol. III is equally explicit about the nature of command and obedience:

To be more specific, domination will thus mean the situation in which the manifested will (command) of the ruler or rulers is meant to influence the conduct of one or more others (the ruled) and actually does influence it in such a way that their conduct to a socially relevant degree occurs as if the ruled had made the content of the command the maxim of their conduct for its own sake. [*E&S*, vol. III, p. 946]

To 'obey' is to become the instrument of another's will. The meaning and content of the obedient subordinates' action becomes the meaning and content of the command executed. This is the social content of the subordinates' action, the purely subjective valuations of the subordinate are irrelevant: 'Furthermore, the fact that it [the command] is so taken is referable only to the formal obligation, without regard to the actor's own attitude to the value or lack of value of the content of the command itself'. [*E&S*, vol. I, p. 215] *The subjective meaning of the subordinate actor is of no account since in obeying he relinquishes the capacity for the social expression of subjective meaning by becoming the instrument of a command.*

In our discussion of the theory of social action we noted that Weber's conception of social relations as reducible to the actions of individual subjects means that it must explain domination as a relation between subjects in which one submits to the other. The *Übermensch* is the true subject of action; the subordinate through submission becomes the means. To submit is to relinquish one's power as a subject, one's will, to another. In the act of obedience, from fear, habit, free will or whatever, the subordinate ceases to be a social subject; the fact of obedience places him below the level of sociological recognition except as a means of action. Sociology is concerned with the true subject of action, the leader whose will, whose ends, are the source of teleological social action. This is true not only of domination but of all complex social relationships. As we shall see, in economic action only managers and consumers (in the case of a capitalist market economy) are economic *subjects*. The workers in production are merely instruments to the realisation of a will and are not, in production, economic subjects. In the economy and in domination only those who can entertain ends or give commands are subjects. The subject once he obeys is only the instrument of a command, and the realm of subjectivity, of will, and autonomous social meaning ends for him when in obeying authority he makes the realisation of 'its' ends his purpose. The subject as subordinate ceases to exist – if he obeys, *why* he obeys is of secondary importance – he becomes a subject only in explicit refusal of command, in revolt.

Further, given the subjectivism of Weberian sociology, there could be no kind of rigorous account of the conditions for compliance. The subject is free to choose whether and why he obeys, his choice is essentially re-created at the moment every command is given. Today's willing dupe may become tomorrow's cynical calculator, the downtrodden wretch in an instant a Spartacus. This subjectivism undercuts itself; the subjective conditions of compliance are clearly important for the quality of obedience yet given the essential freedom of man to choose they can never be known reliably, and, until the subject chooses otherwise, obedience obliterates subjectivity, obedience is ever always formal once one has obeyed. The conditions of compliance are unknowable. The fact of compliance makes the compliant subject unknowable as a subject.

Domination is an inter-subjective relationship, in which one subject submits to the will of another. To attempt to theorise general objective social conditions of existence for this relationship would be contradictory, social relations *are* the interaction of human subjects. The domination relationship explains itself; one subject chooses, for whatever reasons, to obey another. Forms of domination are defined by their *claims* to legitimacy and the structure of organisation deduced from legitimation. Once the forms are defined certain other social relations are associated with them as social concomitants or preconditions, for example, bureaucracy in its rational form presupposes rational laws and a money economy. These ancillary social relations are not conditions of existence of *domination*, however, they say nothing about whether or not domination relationships will exist between subjects. It should also be noted that these ancillary relations are not objective social relations, they too are forms of inter-subjectivity. For example, money exchange and market exchange is a specific form of interaction of human subjects. Superiority and subordination are created by the act of obedience – this is the sole condition of existence of domination that one man accepts another's commands. Domination is a mystery. Why men obey, how men command, is ultimately unknowable. The subjective conditions of compliance cannot be generalised or theorised.

Oppression, subordination to alien and brutal regimes, these real conditions of political power vanish into the relationship of the superior subject and the subordinate subject. State power and politics are mystified in the category of 'domination'. Not only is the content of the category 'domination' mystificatory with respect to political life but its content as a category is mysterious. Social relations are dissolved into inter-subjective relations, and relations between human subjects are dissolved into the mysteries of human 'free will'.

Weber's conception of domination and the role of the claim to legitimacy as the focal point of analysis of forms of rule necessarily exclude democratic forms of rule from serious consideration. This is the case irrespective of the particular arguments advanced against the possibility of genuine democracy (which we will consider later), the categories exclude democratic forms by their very nature. The logic of Weber's categories is as follows:

(i) *Domination* is a relationship of command between leaders and led in which the led are the instruments of the leader's will.

(ii) *Legitimation* is a form of claim of obedience to the leader irrespective of the particular motives of the subject, legitimate domination claims to be worthy of obedience as such.

(iii) Popular rule is excluded by the category of domination – democracy means at best that the people have a means of selection of their leaders and not that they rule on their own behalf.

(iv) Democracy is a form of *legitimation*, it provides a justification for domination by reference to the sanction of the popular will through formal procedures, it is not a form of *rule*. The very notion of popular democracy, that the people rule themselves, or of effective representative democracy, that the representative apparatuses execute the popular will, is excluded by these categories. Such forms, the ideal of the masses of all lands, cannot even be *thought* in Weber's categories.

Modern democracy Weber conceives as an anti-authoritarian transformation of charisma. In this form democracy is *plebiscitary*, the masses acclaim or choose a leader. Weber pointedly insists that the plebiscite is a form of legitimation and that it sanctions the rulers but gives no power to the governed: 'Plebiscitary democracy – the most important kind of *Führer-Demokratie* – is a variant of charismatic authority which hides behind a legitimacy that is *formally* derived from the will of the governed.' [*E&S*, vol. I, p. 268 (emphasis in the original)] Weber is concerned with plebiscitary democracy as a means of *selection* of leaders. In his political writings he is clearly concerned to argue for constitutional, institutional and political arrangements which improve the process of selection of leaders and provide better leadership. This political concern was equalled by Weber's concern that elements of competition be retained in the economy to act as selective mechanisms encouraging and developing entrepreneurial leadership. This political–economic 'interest' is mirrored in the logic of Weber's categories of domination and economic action. Given the subjectivism of Weber's sociology, these leader-figures become essential as the true beings of *will*, the providers *ends*. The *Übermensch* is the source of true social creativity. Other subjects are instrumentalities of these ends. In the modern period the process of rationalisation reinforces the need for leadership. Rationalisation separates the human instrumentalities from the ends they serve, whereas in a less rationalised culture human subjects would be more likely to have religious or ethical cognisance of the ends they served: '. . . rationalisation proceeds in such a fashion that the broad masses of the led merely accept or adapt themselves to the external, technical resultants which are of practical significance for their interests . . . , whereas the substance of the creators' ideas remain irrelevant to them'. [*E&S*, vol. III, p. 1117] The selection of the leadership is, therefore, of more social consequence as greater demands are placed on its quality and creativity.

Leadership is the form in which true human creativity is manifested. Man as a free cultural being exists in the ends and projects of the leaders. Weber's concern with leadership, with the selection of able political and economic leaders with free scope for creative action, is not limited to political and economic 'interests'; it is a concern for the preservation of the free, creative individual. The masses cannot lead and must be led in every sphere, politics, economics, culture, religion. Weber's subjectivism is concerned not with the freedom of *all* human subjects but with the freedom of Man as a cultural being. Culture exists as a realm of human will and purpose even if the mass of humanity submits to the commands of leaders. Weber's starting point, man as the free origin of culture, is not democratic and egalitarian; freedom is an anthropological attribute necessary to a realm of meaning and purpose, not a political category. Weber's anthropology is quite unlike the anthropology of radical humanism. It lacks the insistence of such radical humanists as Rousseau and the young Marx that the potentiality for a free existence, the human essence, which is present in every human subject, be realised in every human subject. Rousseau and Marx seek the abolition of the rule of man by man. Weber is fully prepared to accept the rule of man by man as the condition of creative culture. Mommsen (1965, 1974) is correct to draw attention to the Nietzschean themes in Weber's work. Like Nietzsche Weber accepts the *Übermensch* as the condition of human creativity and purposive culture in a world increasingly dominated by the blind forces of technique. Weber's concern for the human subject is limited to its role as the origin and bearer of culture. The 'transcendental presupposition' of the cultural sciences supports and coexists with a narrowly élitist ideology without the positive and radical libertarianism of the humanist categories of Rousseau and the young Marx.

6

The Sociological Categories of Economic Action

Weber begins his discussion in Chapter II of *Economy and Society* with a disclaimer, that his categories of economic action do not pretend to be an 'economic theory'. Sociology and economics are distinct 'special' social sciences; each has a specific analytically defined aspect of social phenomena to consider. The object of sociology is not that of economics – Weber is not concerned with the *economic* effects of economic relations. Rather, the function of the sociological categories of economic action is to conceptualise economic behaviour in its sociological aspect, to represent economic behaviour as a form of *social* action. These categories therefore examine economic behaviour in terms of its subjective meaning for the actor and the specific nature of the means–ends relationship involved in 'economic' action. Any attempt to provide a substantive analysis of the economic content of economic relations is denied in advance and left to the specialist discipline of economics. Weber's categories cannot, therefore, in his own terms, be criticised for not explaining the economy, for ignoring important aspects of economic relations, or for 'one-sidedness'. They are not an economic theory but a special perspective on economic behaviour. There is no reason why we should accept Weber's own terms. It is necessary to question in particular the very convenient separation of economics and sociology as special social sciences. This separation is another of the methodological devices which enables Weberianism to 'legitimately' ignore the problem of the general relation of the economic level to the social totality. The content of Weber's own work contradicts the methodological protocols he imposes upon it. The separation of economics and sociology is denied by the content of Weber's sociology of economic action. Weber's position in the chapter on economic action does in fact represent a distinct conception of *the economy* and is not simply the consideration of economic behaviour as social action. This conception is closely allied to a definite economic theory.

A SUBJECTIVIST CONCEPTION OF THE ECONOMY

Weber is thoroughly disingenuous in assigning sociology the status of one 'special' social science among others. This 'special' science starts from a general definition of the nature of the social, a definition established by the categories of subjective meaning and social action. 'Special' social sciences can exist so long as they conform to the social ontology of Weber's sociology. An economics which did not consider social action as subjectively meaningful behaviour but as supra-subjective social relations with objective conditions of existence could not coexist with a Weberian sociology. It must become the object of an epistemological critique because it denies the very nature of Weberian sociology's object: social relations as products of the actions of human subjects. And indeed, Weber does reject such an 'economics'; it is called Marxism.

The economics which exists as a parallel social science to sociology must conform to sociology's conception of the social. It must be an economics compatible with the protocols of the theory of social action. Thus there is a definite correspondence between Weber's social categories of economic action and economic theory. Weberian sociology presupposes an economics which explains economic relations as the product of subjectively meaningful action and inter-action of individuals. This economics is represented by the Austrian school of marginalist economic theory (Carl Menger, Eugen von Böhm-Bawerk). Weber adopts Böhm-Bawerk's concept of value and his subjectivist position on the nature of utility (cf. *E&S*, vol. I, p. 69). Weber's defence of capitalism as the most rational economic system because it permits objective calculation of means–ends relations is very similar to the Austrian school's. Böhm-Bawerk (1973) gives a clear statement of this position; Bukharin (1927) and Hilferding (1904) represent powerful Marxist critiques of it.

Weber's theory of social action forces him to conceive economic relations as the product of the purposive action of human subjects. Hence the possibility of 'sociological categories of economic action'; because economic action is purposive human behaviour we can investigate the general subjective character of that behaviour (the purpose of the subject, his conception of it and his conception of the means–ends relationship) independently of its specific 'economic' outcomes and effects. The sociological categories of economic action are primarily a theory of economic *calculation*. Weber is largely concerned in Chapter II with forms of economic calculation and their degree of rationality. This concern with calculation is no accident. Any subjectivist economics requires an ancillary theory of the forms in which the subject represents wants and relates them to the sphere of objective realisation. Calculation is an essential element of the realisation of subjective purpose in the 'economic' sphere; it gives subjective meaning a definite social form (relative to the action of others) and establishes a means–ends relationship.

As with social action in general, 'economic' action is defined by the relation of the subject to his own actions: 'Action will be said to be "economically oriented" so far as, *according to its subjective meaning*, it is concerned with the satisfaction of the *desire* for "utilities"'. [*E&S*, vol. I, p. 63] Action is *not* 'economic' if it is not concerned in a 'subjectively meaningful' way with such questions. Actions cannot be designated as 'economic' independently of the meaning of the subject: '. . . all "economic" processes and objects are characterised as such entirely by the *meaning* they have for human action in such roles as ends, means, obstacles and by-products'. [*E&S*, vol. I, p. 64] What is and is not an economic relation is therefore dependent on the meaning the subject bestows on it. This subjectivism renders any conception of the 'economy' impossible – there is no 'economy' only definite subjectively meaningful behaviours and subjective interactions. The 'economic' would cease to exist as an object for the theory of social action if subjective meanings were no longer attributed to such behaviours. This dependence of the form on the relation of the subject to it is made even clearer in the specific definition of 'economic action': ' "Economic action" is a *peaceful* use of actors control over resources, which is *rationally oriented, by deliberate planning*, to economic ends'. [ibid., loc. cit.] The absence of rational calculation is therefore the absence of economic action. Economic action is nothing but rational action in regard to 'utilities' considered as ends. The economic is designated as an object *subjectively* (subjective meaning of behaviour for actor) and *teleologically* (as utility realising behaviour). What constitutes the unity of the object of economics *and* economic sociology – economic action – as an object of knowledge is the essential similarity of human actions directed towards the satisfaction of the *desire for utilities*.

The unity of this range of behaviours of subjects, which qualifies them for the label 'economic' and to constitute a distinct analytic object, is to be found in the subjective meaning of the actor. Economics is absolutely subjectivised. Classical political economy represented by, for example, Adam Smith, conceived the economic to be a realm of human behaviours directed towards a common end – the satisfaction of *wants*. It unified a set of behaviours as a coherent object of knowledge by ascribing them to a common anthropological origin; these behaviours arise from the wants of man which stem from his being obliged to provide for certain material needs. These needs are objective and follow from man's nature; secondary wants arise on the basis of satisfaction of these needs. Human nature provides the principle of coherence of the facts economic knowledge encounters, it unifies these behaviours (often different in form and the appearances of social custom) and makes economics a universal science (*see* Althusser and Balibar, 1970, ch. 7). Political economy can legitimately deal with beaver hunters and traders on the Baltic Exchange as human subjects engaged in the same activity. Marginalism rejects this anthropological–ontological foundation of economics as a distinct knowledge. Wants are not given. For wants which arise from objective needs are substituted subjective preferences which have no origin except that the subject desires them. For *need* for utilities (man must eat to live, etc.) we have the substitution of *desire* for utilities. This couple *desire–utilities* destroys the notion of utility as deriving from need, or, indeed, as having any objective social form. Utilities become whatever is desired. Desire is limited only by the subjects' preferences, is equivalent to subjective preference itself, and has no conditions of existence other than that the subject decides to prefer it. Utility depends entirely on subjective meaning and subjective preference. It has no objective anthropological form as need, but a different anthropological origin; the subject as a being capable of free choice. *Economic behaviour therefore consists in the satisfaction of those things the subject desires and decides to regard as utilities.*

The 'economic' is reduced to the meanings subjects bestow on certain behaviours. In the absence of such meaning action is not economic. Weber makes this absolutely clear: ' "Economic action" thus is *conscious primary* orientation to economic considerations.

It must be conscious, *for what matters is not the objective necessity of making economic provision*, but the *belief* that this is necessary'. [*E&S*, vol. I, p. 64] Economic action must be conscious action adjusted to the *belief* in the necessity of making economic provision: it follows that the banker in search of his tenth million in the conscious belief that this is necessary is an economic subject while the starving child driven by an 'instinctive search for food' [*E&S*, vol. I, p. 70] is not. It will be recalled that Weber defines econ-omically oriented action by the concern with the satisfaction for the *desire* for utilities. The concept of *desire* creates the space for any-thing to become a 'utility' irrespective of its social usefulness and the concept of '*belief*' in the necessity of making provision for the endless accumulation of resources by certain subjects without objective need. It is not surprising that we find Weber telling us that: 'The definition of "economic action" must . . . be formulated in such a way as to include the operation of a modern business enterprise run for profit.' [*E&S*, vol. I, p. 64] Weber's definition does not just 'include' the capitalist enterprise, it subordinates all other economic forms to the logic of capitalism. Weber's definitions of economic orientation and economic action deliberately *exclude* considerations of social usefulness. Indeed, Weber equates the logic of capitalism and capitalistic calculation with 'formal rationality' in the economic sphere, while considerations of social usefulness are relegated to a different and formally non-rational category 'sub-stantive rationality'.

Weber's conception of economic action as conscious action adjusted to the 'belief' in the 'necessity of making economic pro-vision' and 'rationally oriented by deliberate planning' to that end has certain very definite consequences as to who is and is not an economic subject, as to what behaviours are and are not economic:

(i) It renders all 'economic' behaviour which does not take this form marginal to the category of economic action – this applies to so-called 'Traditional' economic orientation;

(ii) It excludes all wage labourers, slaves and other subordinate workers in their capacity *as producers* from the category of economic subjects;

(iii) The capitalist entrepreneur and the calculating consumer in the capitalist market are the explicit models of 'rational' economic subjects.

Economic action is purposive and it involves deliberate planning of the means to realise the projected ends; economic action is therefore most exactly 'economic' when it corresponds strictly to the general *Zweckrational* action type. Economic subjects are the conscious calculators of the means to empirically realisable ends. Where the end is not explicitly represented and conscious calculation of the most efficient means to its realisation does not take place, then the ensuing behaviour cannot be strictly 'economic action' in the terms of Weber's definition. Weber contends that 'economic *orientation* may be a matter of tradition or of goal-oriented rationality . . .' [*E&S*, vol. I, p. 69], however, economic *action* is not readily compatible with a traditional economic orientation. A traditional economic orientation is one in which the desires for utilities to be satisfied are *given*. Where the ends to be satisfied are *given* it is likely that *given* means will be repeatedly used to achieve the more or less fixed ends. The givenness of the ends provides no mechanism for the systematic rationalisation of the means. A traditional economic orientation does not necessitate the continuing calculation of the most efficient means; 'deliberate planning' can be reduced to the more or less habitual use of given methods to produce a fixed range of utilities. Moreover, the degree to which the given ends are consciously represented is variable, they can be more or less taken for granted. A traditional economic orientation does not of itself give rise to economic action, to 'goal-oriented' rationality. A traditional economic orientation places utility-providing behaviour on the margin of economic action, just as the type of traditional social action defines a form on the 'borderline' of 'meaningfully oriented action'. It follows that the vast mass of the forms of economic provision prior to capitalism, governed by traditional economic orientations, do not qualify as forms of *economic action*. It is capitalism in which we find 'goal-oriented rationality' and, therefore, economic action dominant. Weber's analysis of the necessarily static and conservative character of manufacture governed by a traditional economic orientation will doubtless be recalled from *The Protestant Ethic and the Spirit of Capitalism*. Weber consigns the vast mass of forms of social production to the *pre-history* of economic action.

Economic action is the rational adjustment of means to ends consciously entertained by human subjects. Where labour is hired, or otherwise appropriated, where the subject entertaining the end does not himself produce the utilities in question, subordinate workers enter into production solely as means and not as economic subjects. Weber defines 'labour' thus: 'Human services for economic purposes may be distinguished as (a) "managerial", or (b) oriented to the instructions of a managerial agency. The latter type will be called "labour" for the purposes of the following discussion'. [*E&S*, vol. I, p. 114] The wage workers' activity in producing use values for a capitalist to sell as commodities is a *non-economic* activity; the workers are, either, mere instruments of the managers' orders, or at best limited to technical decisions about methods of production. As a producer the worker is a technical means to an end. The worker can be an economic subject only as a seller of labour power and as a consumer of commodities. It is only in the sphere of consumption that the wage labourer is able to adopt the form of calculation that makes him an economic subject in Weber's terms. A separate managerial agency has the role of economic subject with regard to all forms of production involving a division of labour. Managerial responsibility consists in choosing the means to the realisation of economic ends: '. . . rational orientation is primarily significant for "managerial" action, no matter under what form of organisation'. [*E&S*, vol. I, p. 69]

All economic activity requires a subject who selects the ends of economic action, rationally calculates the most efficient means to realise those ends, and organises the process of realising them. Economic action is rational teleological action. The model forms of such economic subjects are (in the provision of utilities) the capitalist entrepreneur and (in the consumption of ultilities) the consumer who rationally calculates his purchases on the capitalist market. All economic forms entail entrepreneurship. Socialism must have its economic master subjects, its entrepreneurs and managers, just like capitalism. Weber's conception of production as a means to an end chosen by a calculating subject necessarily repeats for all complex forms of production involving a division of labour the separation of the workers from the means of production characteristic of the capitalist enterprise. Socialism cannot dispense with *de facto* entrepreneurship because democratic decision-making is impossible and the leadership, the socialist managers, must make decisions and provide ends for the mass.

It is no accident that capitalism is the most 'rational' economic system for Weber. The conception of economic action as teleological action by subjects cannot but produce this result. The market is the form in which the intersection of such teleologies is possible, in which the projects of 'private' subjects can intersect, into which any subject may enter as buyer or seller, and it is the form which provides a formal means of calculation which establishes an equivalence of the subjects' projects and desires, money.

RATIONALITY AND CAPITALIST CALCULATION

Rationality in the sphere of 'economics' is more or less coincident with 'economic action' – it is the mode in which resources are marshalled by 'deliberate planning' for the most efficient realisation of economic ends. Economic rationality and end-rationality (*Zweckrationalitat*) are identical. Economic rationality is the calculation of the efficiency of means adjusted to the satisfaction of the desire for utilities. *Rationality is a form of calculation.* Weber differentiates between *formal* and *substantive* rationality in economic activity. These are different forms of calculation:

> The term 'formal rationality of economic action' will be used to designate the extent of quantitative calculation or accounting which is technically possible and which is actually applied. The 'substantive rationality', on the other hand, is the degree to which the provisioning of given groups of persons . . . with goods is shaped by economically oriented social action under some criterion . . . of ultimate values, regardless of the nature of these ends. [*E&S*, vol. I, p. 85]

Substantive rationality represents the application of 'ultimate ends' to the measure of economic activity – economic activity is judged by a 'value rational' standpoint. Weber remarks about these 'ultimate ends': 'These points of view are, however, significant only as bases from which to judge the *outcome* of economic action'. [*E&S*, vol. I, p. 86] They do not represent the rational calculation of means to ends, but the evaluative 'calculation' of the results of economic action relative to certain fixed standards. Means–ends calculation is the province of formal rationality. Substantive rationality is therefore a mode in which definite ends are assigned to economic behaviour and a mode of judging the outcome. Only formal rationality can adjust means to ends in terms of efficiency since it provides a quantitative measure of efficiency; a *qualitative* measure of the *efficiency* of use of resources is logically impossible. *All* economic action therefore requires formal rationality and is modelled on formal rationality; resources cannot be 'rationally oriented' to economic ends without quantitative calculation. *The definition of economic action defines it in terms of formal rationality.* Formal and substantive rationality are not alternative and equally 'rational' calculations; end-rational action in the economic sphere requires formal calculation.

What are the conditions of formal rationality in economic action? Formal rationality exists '. . . to the degree in which provision for needs . . . is capable of being expressed in numerical calculable terms, and is so expressed'. [*E&S*, vol. I, p. 85] The units of this calculation may be in money or kind, however, '. . . expression in money terms yields the *highest degree* of formal calculability'. [ibid., loc. cit.] Money calculation and formal rationality are virtually identical. For Weber accounting in money units in terms of profit and loss relative to a free competitive market is the highest form of economic rationality. This form provides precise quantitative comparisons of all resources relative to one another, a purely formal measure of efficiency of resource use (level of profit measured in money units) and a sphere of economic action free of all non-calculable and non-economic factors and limitations.

That monetary calculation, profit and the free market form a constellation necessary to pure formal rationality in economic activity is demonstrated by Weber as follows:

In particular, rational money-accounting presupposes the existence of effective prices and not merely of fictitious prices conventionally employed for technical accounting purposes. This, in turn, presupposes money functioning as an effective medium of exchange, which is in demand as such, not mere tokens used as purely technical accounting units. Thus the orientation of action to money prices and to profit has the following consequences: (1) that the differences in the distribution of money or marketable goods between the individual parties in the market is decisive in determining the direction taken by the production of goods, so far as it is carried on by profit-making enterprises, in that it is only demand made effective through the possession of purchasing power which is and can be satisfied. Further, (2) the question of what type of demand is to be satisfied by the production of goods, becomes in turn dependent on the profitability of production itself. Profitability is indeed *formally* a rational category . . . [*E&S*, vol. I, p. 94]

Money is the most efficient means of calculation: 'From a purely technical point of view, money is the most "perfect" means of economic calculation. That is, it is formally the most rational means of orienting economic activity'. [*E&S*, vol. I, p. 86] Money permits comparative calculation. Calculations in kind are limited to given forms of activity since they provide inventories of stocks, etc., but not means of comparison between goods of a different type. There is no basis of comparison between, say, a million boots and five million hacksaws. Money provides a measure of value in the form of exchange value; if the sale of a million boots yields a profit of £5,000 and the five million hacksaws £1,000, then it is far better to become a boot and shoe manufacturer. Goods are comparable in money terms to the extent that money is the medium of exchange and exchange value dominates social production. Any particular commodity can be expressed in a money form relative to another since both can be purchased with definite quantities of money. The logic of money accounting is the logic of exchange value.

Weber rightly comments that: '. . . money can *never* be merely a harmless "voucher" or a purely nominal unit of accounting so long as it *is* money'. [*E&S*, vol. I, p. 79] Money calculation without markets is not strictly rational accounting since the exchange ratios between goods are determined traditionally or conventionally (cf. *E&S*, vol. I, p. 89) – irrational factors therefore determine exchange ratios. Market exchange and profitability are necessary to the rational calculation of economic alternatives. This is because competition and different returns on resources (profits) make different efficiences of resource use manifest in quantitative terms: 'Rational competition develops only in the case of "marketable goods" and, to the highest degree, when goods are used and sold in a profit system'. [*E&S*, vol. I, p. 74] Competition provides buyers and sellers with explicit quantitative information about the efficiency of resource use in the form of differential prices. The *free* market, limited by no restrictions or combinations, is the form in which money serves most clearly as a measure of efficiency and therefore as an instrument of rational choice between means. The limitation of the freedom of the market produces privileged exchange relationships, and as a result irrationalities and incalculabilities in the form of exchange. Monopolies by being able to affect prices restrict the freedom of other economic actors and therefore the rationality of their choices. The free market is a competition between individuals and not a privileged relationship, the results of the competition between individuals are independent of any particular subject's will. Weber therefore contends: 'Capital accounting in its formally rational shape thus presupposes the battle of man with man'. [*E&S*, vol. I, p. 93]

Money, market-exchange, commodity production and profits are the conditions of formally rational quantitative calculation. Although wage labour is not specified as a necessary condition of formal economic rationality, it is a necessity for the highest form in the logic of Weber's argument. When labour takes a wage form its contribution to production and to the 'costs of production' becomes calculable. The absence of wage labour means that it is impossible to calculate profits and to value the contribution of labour. Economic rationality is defined as capitalist rationality, the rationality of capitalist calculation based on accounting in money terms. All other forms of economic action must be measured as embodying greater or lesser degrees of formal rationality relative to this norm.

Free competition on the market produces the most 'rational' distribution of resources in measured money terms. Weber recognises that this 'rationality' is completely blind to all considerations of social usefulness:

What is to be produced is thus determined, given the distribution of wealth, by the structure of marginal utilities in the income group which has both the inclination and the resources to purchase a given utility . . . the above statement permits us to see the ultimate limitation, inherent in its very structure, of the rationality of monetary economic calculation. It is after all, of a purely formal character. [*E&S*, vol. I, p. 108]

Formal rationality and egalitarianism are necessarily opposed. The economic forms of rational calculation do not produce 'social justice' since they operate through competition to allocate scarce resources. Formal rationality does not necessarily lead to outcomes which substantive rationalities judge acceptable. But no economic system can rationally allocate resources so as to satisfy the substantive criteria of all consumers: 'This is true of consumption in every kind of economic system, including a communist one'. [*E&S*, vol. I, p. 93]

Formal rationality does not lead to 'equality' or 'social justice', it cannot even guarantee full employment or enough to eat for the mass of the people. Because of his distinction between formal and substantive rationality, Weber is often considered to be a critic of capitalism. And so he was, if criticism consists in admitting capitalism is not paradise on earth. Virtually every defender of free market capitalism admits that it is not egalitarian, that it cannot guarantee full employment, etc. Does not Enoch Powell, one of the most determined contemporary defenders of free market capitalism, admit these things? Free market capitalism is defended on the grounds that it is the best system of distribution of resources possible, better than any alternative. Weber follows exactly this line of argument. Indeed, he goes further than this: 'Yet, if the standard used is that of the provision of a certain minimum of subsistence for the maximum size of population, the experience of the last few decades would seem to show that formal and substantive rationality coincide to a relatively high degree'. [*E&S*, vol. I, pp. 108–9] This sounds rather too much like the principle of the greatest happiness of the greatest number to be an accident. It appears that formal rationality does 'maximise' benefits, a familiar apologia for capitalism. Formal rationality because it corresponds to the rational form of teleology makes possible the most efficient *possible* distribution and use of resources. In terms of its own criteria it is justified if it maximises the realisation of the ends of subjects, if it provides resources sufficient for a majority of those subjects who enter the market. Bentham's well-worn catchphrase should not surprise us on Weber's lips, for formal rationality in economic action is nothing but capitalist calculation, and capitalist calculation is the intellectual and social origin of Benthamism. *Formal rationality entails its own substantive rationality*: capitalist calculation leads to the principle of maximisation.

Maximisation is an ethic. Other economic forms than capitalism permit only lower degrees of rational calculability. Poor calculability stems from the privileged determination of resource distribution by extra-economic factors and considerations. Poor calculability in turn promotes arbitrariness and administrative action as means to effect the distribution of resources. Formal rationality is thus substantively justified; the free market maximises benefits *and* personal freedom. In committing himself to what is not simply capitalist calculation but also capitalist *ideology* in his definition of rationality, Weber commits himself to a definite 'substantive' criterion of judgement of the outcomes of economic activity.

Weber's definition of formal rationality in economic activity necessarily force the exclusion of considerations of social usefulness. The reasons for this standpoint follow from the subjectivist conception of the economy. Substantive rationalities cannot allocate resources between different subjective desires for utilities except by evaluative criteria. As human subjects are free to prefer what utilities they will desire there can be no unanimity about the utilities to be satisfied. Someone is bound to be dissatisfied even in a communist society. Where administrative means enter in resource allocation, subordination to authority is also likely to follow. Weber contends: 'But where calculation is only in kind, . . . [the problem of which wants are to be satisfied] is in principle soluble only in one of two ways: by adherence to tradition or by an arbitrary dictatorial regulation which, on whatever basis, lays down the pattern of consumption *and* enforces obedience'. [*E&S*, vol. I, p. 104] Weber's subjectivist definition of the economy necessarily leads to conceiving capitalistic calculation as formal rationality. Weber's conception of the subject as a being of purpose necessarily leads to a subjectivist conception of the economy. The connection of a subjectivist sociology, a marginalist conception of utility and capitalist calculation as formal rationality is a necessary one.

Weber's conception of capitalism as an economic system which is preferable to any other since it minimises administrative action and maximises freedom is a possible one because of a refusal to link economic and political social relations. The capitalist economy can be considered as a pure form of inter-subjective interaction independent of structures of domination.

If we reject Weber's subjectivist theory of utility these objections to allocations of resources in terms of social usefulness fall to the ground. Weber's position depends on subjective preferences being given independently of the mode of distribution. Where this is not the case and essential subjects who prefer on the basis of arbitrary choice are not supposed, then Weber's problem disappears. The utility–desire couple subjectivises demand and makes consumption an entity independent of production. Weber's rejection of considerations of social usefulness depends on accepting the premises of marginalism and of subjectivist sociology. These premises are not inevitable. In the 1857 Introduction and *The Critique of the Gotha Programme* Marx provides cogent arguments for the dependence of consumption on production. These arguments are based on a conception of social relations as objective social forms irreducible to the actions and thoughts of human subjects. Marx demonstrates that consumption and demand are dependent on the system of social production and the relations of distribution which follow from it. Marx argues:

> Any distribution whatever of the means of consumption is only a consequence of the distribution of the conditions of production themselves. The latter distribution, however, is a feature of the mode of production itself. The capitalist mode of production, for example, rests on the fact that the material conditions of production are in the hands of non-workers in the form of property in capital and land, while the masses are only owners of the personal condition of production, of labour power. If the elements of production are so distributed, then the present-day distribution results automatically. If the material conditions of production are the cooperative property of the workers themselves, then there likewise results a distribution of the means of consumption different from the present one. Vulgar socialism . . . has taken over from the bourgeois economists the consideration and treatment of distribution as independent of the mode of production and hence the presentation of socialism as turning principally on distribution. [Marx (1857) *Selected Works*, vol. II, p. 25]

Socialism for Marx is not a matter of distributive justice, nor is socialism an egalitarian system. That a distribution of resources which does not correspond to subjective 'preference' results, that some men are given the same reward for a lower productivity than others, that socialism involves positive discrimination in favour of the proletariat, are not criticisms of socialism for Marx but its necessary concomitants, and, in the case of positive discrimination, its progressive features. Weber's subjectivism is an effective criticism only of theories of distributive justice and absolute egalitarianism, and then again only if the autonomy of 'preferences' is accepted.

Finally, Weber's opposition to criteria of social usefulness depends, in addition to the assumption that preferences in respect of utilities are subjective, on the rejection of the possibility of democratic decision-making and control by the masses. For Weber, Marx's statement that 'the material conditions of production are the co-operative property of the workers themselves' would be meaningless, socialism involves administration and economic leadership which separate the workers from the means of production. Weber's opposition to the idea of popular democracy will be discussed in a later section. We will now consider Weber's characterisation of administration and economic calculation under socialism.

SOCIALISM

We have seen that for Weber money calculation and formal rationality are virtually identical. Calculations in kind are formally rational and possible only when assessing the technical efficiency of different methods of production of a given good or where limited barter exchange takes place between goods 'which are qualitatively similar' [*E&S*, vol. I, p. 101] Accounting-in-kind cannot be formally rational when questions of which types of goods should be produced, which lead to the most efficient use of resources, and of complex distribution of goods are considered. Weber says: 'But more difficult problems of calculation [in kind] begin when it becomes a question of comparing different *kinds* of means of production, their different possible modes of use, and qualitatively different final products'. [*E&S*, vol. I, p. 101] The problems of comparative accounting in kind are almost insuperable, yet such accounting is necessary to socialism, if it aims at replacing the capitalist market and its logic. Rational planning is impossible in a socialist economy:

> Nothing is gained by assuming that, if only the problem of a non-monetary economy were seriously enough attacked, a suitable accounting method would be discovered. The problem is fundamental to any kind of complete socialisation. We cannot speak of a *rational* 'planned economy' so long as in this decisive respect we have no instrument for elaborating a rational plan. [*E&S*, vol. I, p. 103]

Because the problems of accounting in kind cannot be settled, decisions which are the province of comparative accounting, about the relative resource-use efficiency of different products, have to be made on a conventional and non-accounting basis, by tradition or administrative fiat. Socialism is condemned to a formally irrational method of economic decision-making.

The logic of exchange value establishes definite formal equivalences between commodities – they are both capable of being sold for the same sum of money – and a definite criterion of preference between methods of production and commodities to be produced – profitability. Considerations of social usefulness which destroy the conditions of the logic of this system therefore require comparative accounting in kind, but this method is irrational and for all practical purposes impossible. Planned economies must be arbitrary and irrational.

Weber's criticism of socialist accounting is only possible because of the terms in which it is conducted, that is, to discuss the problem of the rationality of planning as if money or stocks were the sole means of calculation available. There is another unit of measurement which does permit comparative accounting, measures of efficiency, and which does not rely on commodity production and exchange as its conditions of existence, that unit is *labour-time*. It is the unit Marx designates as the unit of measurement in a socialist economy in *The Critique of the Gotha Programme*. Labour-time can serve as an accounting unit in the following roles:

(i) As a measure of reward for labour – 'to each according to his work', the principle of distribution in socialism, being calculated in terms of hours of socially necessary labour-time;

(ii) As a measure of the equivalence of goods – the problem of exchange equivalence 'x commodities a, y commodities b' (5 boots = 10 hacksaws?) which is solved in capitalism by exchange value expressed in money, can be solved under socialism by the equivalence of goods directly in terms of the socially necessary labour-time expended on their production;

(iii) As a measure of the efficiency of different processes of production – those processes which reduce the labour-time expended per unit of product will clearly be preferred. Socialist calculation has a unit of measure which can perform the tasks assigned to money accounting in capitalism. Additionally socialist calculation can use inventories as a means of calculating decisions about what quantities of goods are to be produced, large stocks of undistributed goods of a certain type will lead to that sector of production being given a lower periodic target. Socialist planning can express units of labour-time and stocks in conventional money values into the bargain, for the convenience of calculation in personal consumption.

In a socialist economy money may be used as a means of payment for items of personal consumption. However, the prices of goods are not determined by supply and demand but are production prices. In a socialist economy money exchange cannot determine the level of production, its composition, or, to a large extent, its distribution. This is because the level of production in the consumption goods sector (Dept. II) is a function of the supply of producers' goods and the level of production in the producers' goods sector (Dept. I). The relative relation of these two sectors is settled by planning and not by commodity exchange. Thus in the early phases of socialist construction resources may be systematically directed to the expansion of Dept. I and the level of production in Dept. II held down. Planning of this kind is not arbitrary or 'irrational'. The composition of the plan is a function of the elements of production necessary to achieve certain definite targets (thus coal and steel production must expand together).

Planning of this type requires a rational pre-construction of the economic forms to be developed and the calculation of the interrelation of the sectors necessary to achieve this. Planning must take place at the level of the *economy*, achieving the correct balance between sectors. In capitalism planning is only possible at the level of the *enterprise*, the economy being subject to the logics of commodity exchange and capitalist accumulation. Weber's assumption that the market provides the conditions of formal rationality in the form of prices, profits, etc., to which economic activity may be oriented, is nothing more than raising the calculations of the capitalist to the level of a norm for all economic action. It is also absurd. As Charles Bettelheim (1970, 1973) has argued, the prices of commodities are given in any economic system dominated by exchange value. The economy as a whole is subject to the results of commodity exchange, and the price levels, etc., which result from this are the given uncontrollable points of departure of capitalist calculation. Genuine socialism of necessity involves the systematic knowledge of the existing structure of the socialist economy and a rational construction of its future forms. It also supposes genuine democratic discussion of the paths of future development and democratic decision-making in implementation. The calculation of social usefulness without democracy is impossible. While socialism requires scientific knowledge of the economy as a condition of planning, planning is not a scientism; the targets of the plan, the socially useful objects to be produced, must be expressions of the popular will.[1]

In criticising socialism Weber also makes use of the well-worn notions that it weakens incentive for workers and managers alike. Of the incentive to labour Weber says: 'A planned economy

oriented to want satisfaction must, in proportion as it is radically
carried through, weaken the incentive to labour so far as the risk
of lack of support is involved. For it would be impossible to allow
a worker's dependents to suffer the full consequences of his lack
of efficiency in production.' [*E&S*, vol. I, p. 110] Weber would be
less than happy about our so-called 'Welfare State', it would seem.
More importantly, however, Weber assumes that socialism must be
characterised by the very same separation of workers from the
means of production which characterises the capitalist enterprise.
Leaving aside the vexed question of 'moral incentives', Weber simply
ignores the group discipline of the labourers in an enterprise and
its effect on shirkers. Of incentives to managers, Weber remarks:
'Furthermore, autonomy in the direction of organised productive
units would have to be greatly reduced or, in the extreme case
eliminated. Hence it would be impossible to retain capital risk and
proof of merit by a formally autonomous achievement'. [ibid., loc.
cit.] This is simple nonsense. Enterprises under central planning
have to meet certain plan targets. Failure to do so provides a
definite minimum limit of performance. The differential consumption
of labour-time, raw materials, etc., between enterprises can lead
to efficient enterprises being rewarded and their performance being
made the norm for the others. Central control and the absence of
workers' control does lead to waste, overstocking and the accumulation of labour reserves as a guarantee against shortages and failure
to meet plan targets in the Soviet Union, but this reveals not an
absence of incentive on the part of managers, rather a particularly
inefficient response to the incentives to performance imposed by
plan targets.

As we have seen, Weber maintains that socialism involves the
separation of the workers from the means of production and
decision-making. This is because of Weber's conception of 'economic
action'. The realisation of the end is impeded if workers do not
simply participate as means but attempt to take a part as subjects,
producing cross-cutting subjectivities and irrationalities:

. . . it is generally possible to achieve a higher level of economic
rationality if the management has extensive control over the selection and modes of use of workers, as compared with the situation
created by the appropriation of jobs or the existence of rights to
participate in management. These latter conditions produce

technically irrational obstacles as well as economic irrationalities. [*E&S*, vol. I, p. 138]

A system of socialist production in which the workers were *not* separated from the means of production would therefore be even more irrational for Weber. Rational decision-making consigns the workers to the status of means, it assigns them to 'modes of use'. Democratic decision-making at the social level, establishing standards of social usefulness, democratic decision-making at the level of the enterprise, producing worker motivation and the creative transformation of the relation of the labourer to his work which revolutionises the productivity of labour, are impossible in a socialist or any other society according to Weber. Weber denies that socialism is an economic system based on the rational planning of resources or that it develops the forces of production, in both these respects socialism is inferior to capitalism.

7

The Critique of Popular Democracy

It has been argued that Weber's types of legitimate domination exclude popular democratic rule from consideration and that the impossibility of democratic decision-making is central to Weber's critique of socialism. In this section we will consider Weber's arguments as to *why* democratic decision-making and popular rule are impossible in all but the most simple societies.

In *Economy and Society* Weber considers democratic *rule* as an extreme case, existing only in small relatively primitive societies. It is an historical anomaly. Direct democracy, in which the people regularly and exclusively take part in administration, is the sole form of democratic *rule*. Direct democracy exists where the following conditions are met:

> . . . (1) the organisation must be local or otherwise limited in the number of members; (2) the social positions of the members must not greatly differ from each other; (3) the administrative functions must be relatively simple and stable; (4) however, there must be a certain minimum development of training in objectively determining ways and means. [*E&S*, vol. III, p. 949]

Direct democracy is confined to circumstances such as the relatively isolated and primitive peasant village. Once the organisation passes beyond a certain maximum size and a measure of social differentiation takes place, then direct democracy turns into the rule of notables. Weber says of direct democracy: 'We must not look, however, upon this kind of administration as the historical starting point for any typical course of development but rather as a marginal type case.' [ibid., loc. cit.] With direct democracy ends rule *by* the people.

Size and the complexity of administrative tasks are the principal determinants of the need for non-popular specialist administration.

A specialist administration separates the mass of the people from administrative performance, administrative competence and the means of administration. The people become the objects of administration without access to the administrative machinery. This separation from the means of administration radically changes the nature of 'democracy'. Representative democracy is not popular control. Democracy changes its nature from a mode of administration to, at best, a mode of selection of the leadership: 'As soon as mass administration is involved the meaning of democracy changes so radically that it no longer makes sense for the sociologist to ascribe to the term the same meaning as in the case discussed so far.' [*E&S*, vol. III, p. 951]

Democracy ends because certain persons become leaders and control the means of administration. The leadership is not only not directly controllable by the people, but it does not have the same interests as the people. It develops specific interests attaching to its position of power. The end of rule by the people is also the end of rule *for* the people. Leadership is the end of democracy because the leadership necessarily does not represent the interest of the people. Representative democracy cannot be popular democracy, whatever its constitutional form. Democracy ends wherever there is leadership. Weber follows Michels in coupling the irresponsibility of the leaders to the masses with the displacement of the goals of the masses. Weber's position – uncontrollable and self-interested leadership created by the need for specialist administration as a result of the size and complexity of the activities to be administered – is identical in form and content to Michels' 'Iron Law of Oligarchy'.

Leadership, of one kind or another, is a permanent fact in all complex organisations. The masses have no control over the leadership in general because if they help to replace a given leadership they install another equally uncontrollable and with the same monopoly of administrative means. Whether this transition is peaceful, through election, or violent, through revolution, the people do not control – democratically elected leadership is as irresponsible to the people as the leadership of a revolutionary *coup d'état*. The demos can never prevail against an entrenched leadership without replacing it with another. This inevitability of élites is a function of what Weber calls the 'law of the small number':

The predominance of the members of such a structure of domination rests upon the so-called 'law of the small number'. The ruling minority can quickly reach an agreement among its members; it is thus able at any time to initiate that rationally organised action which is necessary to preserve its position of power. Consequently it can easily squelch any action of the masses threatening its power as long as the opponents have not created some kind of organisation for the planned direction of their struggle for domination. [*E&S*, vol. III, p. 952]

This general inevitability of elites is reinforced in modern societies by the predominance of the bureaucratic form of administation. The 'law of the small number' is magnified in its effects by the fact that bureaucracy is the most rational form of administration, it provides the most efficient calculation of the means–ends relationship and the most reliable form of execution of given tasks. It therefore provides the most efficient means of repression. Bureaucracy is administration by competent specialist officials operating through written documents within a framework of rational rules. Where complex activities have to be coordinated bureaucratic administration is essential – this is because in its rational form it provides reliability, continuity and calculability in decision-making. Bureaucracy emphasises the separation of the masses from the means of administration: it entails the administration of the activities of the masses by permanent career officials who are not responsible to the public and who employ administrative rules and criteria which are based upon specialist knowledge not accessible to the public.

Bureaucratic administration is ubiquitous in and indispensible to modern social life, in the economic, political and cultural realms. It is dominant because the complex division of labour which is necessary to the social institutions of modern capitalism could not continue to exist without coordinating and supervising agencies of the type. Bureaucracy is objectively necessary to the welfare of the ruled:

The ruled, for their part, cannot dispense with or replace the bureaucratic apparatus of authority once it exists. For this bureaucracy rests upon expert training, a functional specialisation of work, and an attitude set for habitual and virtuoso-like mastery of single yet methodically integrated functions. If the official stops working, or if his work is forcefully interrupted, chaos results, and it is difficult to improvise replacements from among the governed who are fit to master such chaos. This holds for public administration as well as for private economic management. More and more the material fate of the masses depends upon the steady and correct functioning of the increasingly bureaucratic organisations of private capitalism. The idea of eliminating these organisations becomes more and more utopian. [*E&S*, vol. III, p. 988]

The 'needs of mass administration' make bureaucracy 'completely indispensible'. [*E&S*, vol. I, p. 223] Even if the masses sought to throw off the bureaucratic yoke and succeeded they would be acting against their own interests – not only does bureaucracy provide the most efficient means of social control but the best standard of material well-being available.

Why is bureaucracy superior to other forms of administration? Weber answers as follows:

The primary source of the superiority of bureaucracy lies in the role of technical knowledge which, through the development of modern technology and business methods in the production of of goods have become completely indispensible. In this respect it makes no difference whether the economic system is organised on a capitalistic or a socialistic basis. [*E&S*, vol. I, p. 223]

Bureaucracy rules through rational calculation of the means–ends relationship. It is more efficient in calculation because, in its rational form, all non-rule-governed elements have been eradicated from it. Rational bureaucratic administration reduces to a minimum the arbitrariness and irregularity inherent in other forms of administration. In reducing its own action to a calculable form it makes possible rational calculation in respect of the activities to be administered.

Bureaucracy entails the concentration and separation of the means of administration on an unprecedented scale. Not only are the masses separated from the control of administrative activities but all kinds of 'notables' are also. Bureaucracy reduces the politician to an administrative 'dilettante'. Technical knowledge, as the primary means of administration, is appropriated by the bureaucracy and becomes secret knowledge. Rational calculation in administrative tasks is interiorised within the bureaucratic machine, it becomes the province of specialists selected, trained and controlled by the bureaucracy. Monetary calculation is *public*, the conditions of calculability are available to every consumer, administrative calculation is the property of bureaucrats.

The administrative machine is able to prevail in the regular conduct of affairs over elected, or other, political leaders. This is because in contrast to the politician it has continuity in office and because it is possessed of technical knowledges which it monopolises and converts into secrets. However, bureaucratic administration is blind. It administers the application of means but it cannot, as administrative calculation, devise ends. Bureaucratic administration will operate on any given ends which are empirically realisable. Creative leadership is needed to provide the ends of administrative action. This leadership, as we have seen, is provided in politics by the plebiscitary leader and in the economy (whether capitalist or socialist) by the entrepreneur.

In modern societies Weber argues that bureaucratic state administration tends to be combined with *plebiscitary democracy*. This occurs wherever the masses enter into politics and formal democracy exists. Mass politics leads to the plebiscitarian principle on two levels. The first level is that of the political party. Mass parties are bureaucratic parties – the political *apparat* exists to mobilise voters. The party machine promotes and acclaims its 'charismatic' leadership. Bureaucracy and the demagogic leader are combined as the dual conditions of electoral success. The second level is that of the state apparatus. The dominance of the bureaucracy within the state reduces political notables and parliamentarians to the role of salaried lobby fodder and elevates the elected head of the state apparatus to primacy. Plebiscitary democracy is not genuine popular representation. At best the people choose between leaders preselected for them by bureaucratic party machines. At most plebiscitarian 'democracy' is a form in which the masses acclaim the existing authorities.

Weber's critique of democracy as a form of popular rule rests on two main arguments:

(i) The 'law of small numbers';
(ii) The dominance of bureaucratic administration as a function of its technical necessity.

Weber's 'law of the small number' supposes that the leadership forms a stratum distinct from the masses with its own special interests antagonistic to those of the masses. The 'law of the small number' is a variant of Michels' 'Iron Law of Oligarchy':

By a universally applicable law, every organ of the collectivity, brought into existence through the need for a division of labour, creates for itself, as soon as it becomes consolidated its own particular interests. The existence of these special interests involves a necessary conflict with the interest of the collectivity. [Michels (1962), p. 353]

Leadership or representation of any kind must lead to the displacement of the interests of the masses. No proofs whatever are offered by Weber or Michels for the 'universal applicability' of this proposition. The very fact of leadership makes popular democratic control impossible. Any leadership is not subject to the control of the people and develops separate interests from them. Replacing one leadership with another leads to no advantage for the masses. The 'Iron Law' involves two propositions:

 (i) *Irresponsibility* – the leadership cannot be controlled by the masses;
(ii) *The displacement of interests* – the leadership seek to retain power in their own interests, these interests are inimical to those of the masses.

There is no reason why (ii) follows from (i), or why (i) should apply at all.

The very fact that the people may replace one leadership with another provides the incumbent leadership with a reason for complying with popular demands. If the threat of replacement is effective it provides both a measure of popular control and a means of ensuring that popular demands are met at least in part. Regimes are less responsive to popular demands the less vulnerable they are to popular pressure. Where representation takes the form of short terms of office on delegate committees, the delegates being subject to recall, and where cohesive basic units from which delegates are elected exist, then popular control is real and significant. Leadership and representation may be necessary above the most basic levels of self-administration, but they do not inevitably lead to forms beyond popular control. This is true of the state apparatuses of the nation state – the more administration is open to inspection, to agencies of popular pressure, and to free public discussion, the greater the degree of popular control. Theories which stress the inevitability of irresponsible leadership are political ideologies directed against struggles for democratisation and popular control. Weber and Michels' 'Iron Law' is reminiscent of another – Lassalle's 'Iron Law of Wages'. Both laws have the same effect if their 'universal applicability' is accepted, they inhibit the masses from fighting for better conditions.

Weber and Michels provide no proofs for the notion that all forms of leadership must inevitably become irresponsible to the masses irrespective of the forms of popular control imposed on them. Furthermore, for Weber and Michels all forms of irresponsibility are equivalent, from the tendency of delegate committees to act without direct reference to their constituents to the most oppressive military dictatorships. It is the pure ideal of popular control which is being challenged. Once direct democracy gives way to leadership Weber loses all interest in questions of popular control. Weber and Michels are indifferent to the *degrees* of popular control and public accountability which are possible within different forms of representation and administration. Direct democracy, a notion to be relegated to the level of the parish council, and domination are the sole alternatives. Yet the space between authoritarian domination and non-specialist self-administration is the arena of struggle for democratic theory and practice. In asserting the inevitability of domination Weber abandons any serious attempt to challenge democracy. The 'laws' of Weber and Michels turn out to have less ferrous content than they imagined.

The linking of the propositions of irresponsibility and the displacement of interests is even less justified. Organisations which are not subject to popular control are not beyond popular pressure or the passive resistance of the people. An organisation which acts in direct contradiction to the interests of its members, for example a trade union which makes no reasonable effort to raise wage levels and improve working conditions while paying its officials vast salaries, will suffer from desertions, refusals of funds, and from a lack of popular support. A certain level of performance of the basic tasks desired by the membership is a condition of support in respect of organisations like capitalist enterprises and their shareholders, or unions and their members. Weber's anti-democratism reveals how little stress he places on the conditions of compliance. The same considerations apply to nation states. Mobilisation of support, essential in wars, civil wars and economic crises, is not possible without widespread concessions to popular demands.

Weber's general critique of the possibility of democratic control, 'the law of the small number', is complemented by his insistence that bureaucratic administration is indispensible in modern societies. Bureaucracy renders popular democratic control impossible for three main reasons:

(i) It is technically superior to the 'dilettante' forms of administration which would be inevitable under popular control;
(ii) It involves centralisation, and centralisation is both a necessary consequence of modern mass social forms and an obstacle to popular control;
(iii) The necessity of coordination which results from a complex division of labour requires specialist administrative personnel.

Let us consider these arguments in turn.

Bureaucracy is technically superior to other forms of administration because it makes possible rational calculation in administration. 'Technical knowledge' is the basis for the 'dictatorship of the official' (cited in Beetham, 1974, p. 71). Weber recognises that the knowledge on which the power position of the official rests is of two kinds: specialist technical knowledge, and 'official' knowledge, knowledge of the procedures of the bureaucracy which is a secret of the *apparat* (*see* Beetham, 1974, p. 74). In the case of the first type of knowledge there is no reason why it should not be widely available to the people through public education and information. Technical knowledge, of engineering, jurisprudence, medicine, etc., can be made public knowledge. Firstly, by a popular higher education not restricted to specialist cadres; cadres who enjoy a privileged and well-rewarded career precisely because such knowledges are in scarce supply. Secondly, by programmes of general information designed to acquaint the masses in a non-specialist way with the content and effects of various knowledges. 'Technical knowledge' is kept a mystery for the mass of the people because no attempt is made to develop the educational system which would make it *public* knowledge. In the case of the second type of knowledge it is simply a function of the existence of administrative apparatuses to which the people do not have free access. Thus agencies like the Department of Health and Social Security operate through secret administrative procedures and decide on cases by means of criteria which are not public and subject to little effective popular scrutiny.

To suppose that such agencies are technically superior to popular forms of administration in such areas as welfare, health and education is highly questionable. A social 'security' system which operated through simple published rules and by means of popular tribunals (subject to appeal) would, even under existing conditions, probably improve the lot of those in need of public aid and the efficiency of its distribution. Popular administration need not be on the basis of the 'substantive' prejudices of the masses as Weber believes – there is no reason why popular administration should not be rule-governed. Popular administration would improve the flow of information about the conditions and needs of the administered. Many of the difficulties in the operation of the social security system are the result of the ignorance and fear on the part of claimants, and the suspicion on the part of officials, created by bureaucracy itself.

Formal rationality in administration consists in making the actions of the bureaucracy calculable, or rather, its *internal* administrative effects calculable. This form of calculability necessarily conditions administration of this type to resistance to frequent changes of policy, such changes require revisions of the rules and procedures to ensure calculability. Administrative calculability pertains to the structure of the organisation in question and its operation and not to the activities administered or their operation. These activities are part of the general realm of means–ends calculation; this calculation need not be undertaken by bureaucracies. The separation of the masses from the means of administration necessary for bureaucracy also entails the separation of the bureaucrat from the masses. This has a dual effect: the bureaucrat proceeds in ignorance of the conditions and needs of the masses, and the masses are unable to intervene effectively in administration to verify errors in calculations. This must necessarily limit the effectiveness of means–ends calculation by bureaucratic agencies. Further, the greater the calculability of the operation of the administrative machine the less it can respond to rectify its own errors in means–ends calculation.

Weber's bureaucracy is claimed to be technically more efficient than *previous* forms of administration. Weber makes no attempt to show that it is technically superior to forms of administration which combine rule-governed action, technical knowledge and popular participation. He dismisses the very idea. Bureaucracy is based on specialist knowledge. The intervention of the masses, 'existence of rights to participate in management', tends to 'technically irrational obstacles'. The masses, whether as workers or objects of administration for state welfare and other agencies, play their part best if they do what they are told. The worker's part in production is as a means to an end; auotonomous action by the workers reduces their calculability as means with a precise type of action and therefore upsets the calculability of the means–ends relation. The administered's part in administration is to follow the commands of the officials, otherwise deviations from the calculated course of action might result. The masses do not have the specialist knowledge to do anything but harm, their substantive interests impede formal rationality. The idea that popular education could provide every worker with a degree in some branch of engineering or that a socialist society might compel bureaucrats and Heidelberg professors to do manual work and to accept workman's wages never enters Weber's head. That the result might be an infinitely more 'rational' system of production is unthinkable for him.

Why centralisation should impede democratic control is difficult to see. Rousseau favoured the elimination of local and secondary associations, the creation of a unitary state, in order to permit the popular will to be expressed without the influence of particular 'interests' and in order to prevent the formation of means of subversion of popular rule. Marx in *The Civil War in France* argued that the communal constitution represented a unified and centralised nation state and not a federation. If the friends of liberty have argued for centralisation, it is because they have argued for a quite different form from that of the centralised state operating through administrative apparatuses beyond popular control. Thus the communal constitution represented a national unity based on *communes*, upon popular executive–legislative bodies in towns and regions, and not a unity of the state administration of a uniformly subordinate and politically inert countryside. The centralisation of information and control, the concentration of functions in executive–legislative bodies, favours the control by the popular masses. The separation of legislation and execution, the existence of numerous agencies of administration and state power, limits the effectiveness of popular intervention. For example, those states least subject to the threat of popular action are those with complex and overlapping agencies of state security. The neo-Bonapartist regime in France has less to fear from the loyalty of the conscript army because it has several 'parallel' security forces, with distinct heirarchies, ministerial power bases and which are insulated from popular influence or control. A country with a militia army organised on a democratic basis and no other security agencies would necessarily have a government more subject to popular pressure. Centralisation is not necessarily an obstacle to popular control.

Weber is indeed correct that where there is a complex division of labour there is a need for specialist functions of coordination. Marx calls the functions of coordination made necessary by the *technical* division of labour a 'productive job'. [Marx, 1894, III, p. 376] He contrasts such necessary labour of coordination with the supervision work made necessary by a *social* division of labour which separates workers from the means of production. Weber supposes the combination of the two functions – he assumes the necessity of the separation of the worker from the means of production as the condition of rational coordination. Yet we may state the following thesis: the more antagonistic the separation between manager and managed, the greater the labour devoted to supervision and the less efficient the means of coordination. This thesis illustrates the 'irrationality' of managerialism, whether of a Weberian or other kind. It is not a 'utopian' thesis – part of the 'dream' of socialism – it could be a practical axiom of rational capitalist business administration concerned with the achievement of high and uniform rates of production rather than with dictatorial control. Progressive managements have attempted to reduce the labour of supervision, to minimise differentiations between workers in terms of functions, wage-levels, and incentives. The necessary consequence of the formation of functional groups within the plant, interchangeability of tasks, etc., is greater practical control of the activity of producing by the workers. Seymour Melman's excellent and neglected study of the Standard Motor Company, *Decision Making and Productivity*, demonstrates these facts admirably and stands as a condemnation of the production and supervision policies adopted or continued by managements in the British motor industry since it was written.

The calculation of the conditions necessary for complex processes of production is possible only if those whose tasks are to be co-ordinated understand and cooperate. No complex process can work efficiently unless information is regularly relayed back about the operation of its parts and minor adjustments are constantly made as errors or stoppages occur. Where the workers do not actively co-operate then supervision on an extensive scale is necessary; this raises the costs of production and reduces the effectiveness of reaction to obstacles. The antagonistic separation of workers and managers is what causes 'technically irrational obstacles'. In contradiction to Weber, efficiency is only possible when the production workers do *not* play the part of cogs in a wheel. Socialism based upon genuine popular ownership (where the workers are not separated from possession of their enterprises) and plant self-management is the sole condition of this antagonism being reliably overcome. This creative participation of the workers in production is a large part of what Marx means when he says that socialism develops the 'forces of production'.

Coordination work would still be a necessity under socialism, but it does not mean that the technical functionaries in question must therefore have the power to give merely obedient workers orders. Given democratic plant management by a delegate committee, effective public education and widespread technical training, the regular rotation of personnel – there being no such thing as a professional manager – then the function of coordination need not be the source of any special stratum of functionaries. The correlate of Lenin's aphorism 'even a cook can learn to govern' is that even a guv'nor can learn to cook. Weber's technical specialists are elevated above the people precisely because a class society denies the mass of the people effective participation in decision-making in production and in general administration, denies them higher education, the leisure for culture and political knowledge. This same class society creates privileged cadres of 'officials' and 'specialists' to meet necessary administrative functions – enjoying education and wages far above those of the mass of the people. 'Socialist' societies in which these cadres exist are a record of the degree of failure to overcome the conditions imposed by capitalist class society. Yet, even within modern capitalist society, less repressive and authoritarian forms of administration and more democratic forms of government are possible. The ultra-left adopt the reversed mirror image of Weber's position, they conceive that capitalism 'needs' authoritarian forms and that democratic institutions and civil liberties are merely a screen to hide the realities of oppression. This is merely to do the anti-democrats' work for them. Thinkers like Marcuse are the most effective anti-democratic ideologists because they sap the struggle for more democratic forms from what appear to be radical left positions. In contradiction to Weber, Marcuse, the elitist and managerial ideologues, more democratic forms of administration and representation are possible in contemporary capitalist social formations. The greater the experience of the masses in administration, the more effective programmes of popular education, and the more genuine public political discussion, then the better the chance that from such capitalist conditions a progressive and popular socialism can be constructed rather than one frozen in the insuperable obstacles of transition.

In this chapter the political positions present in *Economy and Society* have been challenged by other and opposed political positions. This is a very different practice from the logical and conceptual critique in the earlier chapters. Two things should be made clear in this respect:

(i) That the theoretical critique is not reducible to this political critique or to the author's 'motives' in challenging Weber's sociological categories – whether it is right or wrong is a strictly theoretical matter;

(ii) Likewise Weber's epistemological and sociological categories are not simply the form of manifestation of certain political interests'. *Economy and Society* is not a coherent whole: it is neither united as the emanation of the mind if its 'author', embodying a distinct personal–political 'outlook', nor is it united as the realisation of its most basic (epistemological) categories, its politics being a simple extension of its theory. Indeed, the categories of *Economy and Society* themselves undercut the possibility of such simple connections between theory and politics. The radical relativism and personalism of Weberian epistemology inevitably lead to the conclusion that the types of domination and the economic sociology developed in *Economy and Society* represent *only one possible set of categories*, rational extensions of a certain set of values. This means that other sets are claimed not only to be possible but also of equivalent validity; thus an anarchist could adopt this epistemology and embody anarchist values in different categories. The claim is in part true, there *are* radical Weberians. It is, however, a misleading truth, and it depends on the acceptance of the Weberian epistemology (that is, knowledge depends on the incorporation of prior values into ideal types). The more specific categories in *Economy and Society* could be changed in content without their contradicting the more general categories which define the nature of social knowledge and social action, but only if these changed categories were capable of bearing the burden of relativism and personalism this discourse imposes. This burden stems from the constitution of the human subject's actions as the object of knowledge and the simultaneous insistence that this subject's freedom is the unpassable and unquestionable frontier of knowledge.

8

Conclusion

These two studies have attempted to demonstrate the dependence of forms of classification on the concepts and questions of definite theories. In this discussion we have questioned the status of classifications, not in order to deny the need for rigorous typifications of social forms, but in order to challenge the widely held idea that classifications are independent formal schemas which may be more or less 'convenient' or 'useful' to the researcher in ordering his material. Classification and typification are a part of theory, and not practices independent of it.

It will be evident that the author does not regard the theoretical positions considered in this book, the variants of 'social evolutionism' and Weber's sociological categories, as an adequate basis for the analysis of social relations. Space prevents a discussion of alternatives in this work. In *Pre-Capitalist Modes of Production* Barry Hindess and I have attempted to consider in some detail the Marxist theory of modes of production. In that work we attempted to avoid teleological formulations of the concepts of modes of production. Such concepts, in which social relations are the product of or the means of realisation of a purpose, have dominated Marxist theory. The effect of such concepts is to make history a necessary hierarchy, to define social relations by the place they are assigned in this hierarchy, for example, feudal social relations are conceived so as to explain or necessitate the development of capitalism, or, capitalism is conceived in terms of the mechanisms of its anticipated demise. Such teleologies impose on knowledge the limitations of a purpose or of a pre-given hierarchy of forms.

The classification of social relations in historicist Marxism follows the order of hierarchy of its process of history. The classifications we have considered in this book are also ordered by teleologies. Spencer's classification of social institutions forms a hierarchy within the greater hierarchy of progress, the move from homogeneity to heterogeneity reflects the general direction of evolution of the cosmos. Weber's individualistic and relativisitic typifications of social action both purport to explain social relations as the product of the purposive action of individuals and are limited as knowledge by the insistence on the freedom of action of individuals. In this theory all necessities of connection between phenomena and all relations of consistency between explanatory categories are subverted by a radical personalism.

Spencer and Weber reflect opposed and, in their own ways, rigorous practices of grounding and justifying purpose. Spencer subordinates the whole of nature to a single teleology; nothing escapes, and therefore nothing non-purposive can subvert, this universal evolution towards an end. Weber makes the human subject the unquestionable source of meaning and purpose. Whether these purposes are realised or not is a secondary question. Man is free to entertain purposes and because of this he is free in a way that makes his essence and his future actions ultimately unknowable. In the one case all knowledge is subordinated to the (empty) principles of a universal science. In the other the possibility of general and objective explanations of social relations is denied.

It should not be thought that the question of teleological action is simply being dismissed here. Clearly, human subjects do, at the level of 'conscious thought' (a problematic notion) devise projects and seek to realise certain states of affairs. Clearly, political agencies and movements seek to bring about certain states of affairs. There is a vast difference, however, between recognising teleological elements in social practice as an object to be problematised and explained, and constructing explanations of social relations in terms of teleology. But, it may be asked, what is wrong with teleological explanations? Teleological explanations involve the necessitation of purpose or of hierarchies of forms; these necessitations cannot be conditional if the teleology is to be a rigorous one, if it is not to be subverted (rendered non-teleological) by the effects of exterior conditions. This non-conditional necessity imposes itself in the form of the universalisation of teleology (Hegel, Spencer) or in irrationalism and personalism (Kierkegaard, Weber). Positions of this kind demonstrate clearly the dependence of classifications on theories.

Notes

Chapter 2

1 Spencer did not conceive his position as teleological. Because progress is an objective process involving all nature Spencer thinks he has defined progress non-teleologically. Spencer means by teleology: either, explanations based upon human wills or needs (x exists because it is necessary for man) or, where a direction is ascribed to the effect of some supernatural force (hence he attacks Erasmus Darwin and Lamarck). Teleology for Spencer means purpose related to will rather than any process which works in a certain direction to realise an end. Despite this Spencer's position is teleological – teleology is essential to any conception of *progress*. Adaptation alone cannot guarantee a definite directionality: Spencer 'is still obliged to smuggle teleology in by back ways since, because he wants to demonstrate history's inevitable path to perfection, he needs a guarantee of direction in evolution. This cannot be provided by adaptation, since that provides no account of how the environment may change.' [Peel (1971) p. 135]

2 In fact the method by which Terray demonstrates that there are 'similarities' with Darwin is exactly the same as the one he uses to demonstrate 'correspondences' with Marx. It should be noted that Terray's method of analysis of texts is exactly the one Althusser argues against in *Reading Capital*. This method abstracts concepts from their problematic and uses one problematic (Darwin, Marx) as a *grid* to read and recognise the concepts of another (Morgan).

Chapter 3

1 Values are *rationalisable* – their consequences for conduct may be logically drawn out, and conduct may be adjusted to certain rules derived from these values irrespective of the results (c.f. the category of *Wertrational* action). This rationalisation pertains to the logic and consequences of values, and to the means–ends relation, the *content* of the values in question is not thereby made rational.

2 Weber conceives explanations entirely in terms of a factorial theory of history. Explanation involves determining the factors operative in an 'event' and weighing their causal significance. Ideal-types are used in this 'explanatory' process: general theory, or the attempt to explain the conditions of existence of social relations are impossible. Only concrete unique events, persons and ideas are real and worthy of study – historical explanation treats the 'factors' entering into an event as given to be assessed relative to the event and not explained in themselves.

Chapter 5

1 There is no significant theoretical difference between the two drafts of the three types of domination text printed in *Economy and Society*. The first version (written later) in Vol. I has been used predominantly here, but the second (written before the first) in Vol. III is cited and quoted supplementary to it and it will be seen that it agrees with the first on all major points.

Chapter 6

1 Our discussion of socialist planning is abstract, it is pitched at the same level of generality as Weber's. Problems of calculation and planning in socialist countries have produced a vast literature; notable in this respect are attempts by serious socialist economists to argue the role of a modified market mechanism in such economies; *see* W. Bruz (1972) and E. G. Liberman (1970).

Bibliography

Althusser, Louis and Balibar, Etienne, *Reading Capital* (London, New Left Books, 1970).

Beetham, David, *Max Weber and the Theory of Modern Politics* (London, George Allen & Unwin, 1974).

Bettelheim, Charles, *Calcul économique et formes de propriété* (Paris, François Maspero, 1970).

Bettelheim, Charles, 'State Property and Socialism', *Economy and Society*, Vol. 2, No. 4 (1973). (A translation of pp. 67–92 of the above.)

Böhm-Bawerk, Eugen von, *Value and Price* (an excerpt from *Capital and Interest*) (South Holland, Illinois, Libertarian Press, 1973).

Bruz, W., *The Market in a Socialist Economy* (London, Routledge & Kegan Paul, 1972).

Bukharin, Nikolai, *Economic Theory of the Leisure Class* (1927) (Reprinted New York, Monthly Review Press, 1972).

Burrow, J. W., *Evolution and Society* (Cambridge, Cambridge University Press, 1966).

Coleman, W. R., *Georges Cuvier* (Cambridge, Mass., Harvard University Press, 1964).

Collins, F. Howard, *Epitome of the Synthetic Philosophy* (a summary of Spencer's *Synthetic Philosophy*) (London, Williams & Norgate, 1894).

Darwin, Charles, *The Origin of Species* (1859) (ed. J. Burrow) (Harmondsworth, Penguin, 1970).

Dilthey, Wilhelm, *The Essence of Philosophy* (1954) (Reprinted, New York, A.M.S. Press, 1969).

Dilthey, Wilhelm, *Pattern and Meaning in History* (New York, Harper & Row, 1962).

Engels, Frederick, *The Origin of the Family, Private Property and the State* (1884) (London, Lawrence and Wishart, 1972).

Glass, B., Temkin, O. and Strauss, W. (eds), *Forerunners of Darwin 1745–1859* (Baltimore, Johns Hopkins, 1959).

Hilferding, Rudolf, *Böhm-Bawerk's Criticism of Marx* (1904) Reprinted in P. M. Sweezy (ed.), *Karl Marx and the Close of his System* (New York, Augustus M. Kelly, 1949).

Hindess, B. and Hirst, P. Q., *Pre-Capitalist Modes of Production* (London, Routledge & Kegan Paul, 1975).

Hodges, H. A., *The Philosophy of Wilhelm Dilthey* (London, Routledge & Kegan Paul, 1952).

Hodges, H. A. *Wilhelm Dilthey. An Introduction* (London, Routledge & Kegan Paul, 1969).

Kolko, Gabriel, 'A Critique of Max Weber's Philosophy of History', *Ethics*, Vol. 70, pp. 21–36 (1959).

Liberman, E. G., *Economic Methods and the Effectiveness of Production* (1970) (New York, Anchor Books, 1973).

Lukács, Georg, *Die Zerstörung der Vernuft* (1955) (Werke 9, Luchterhand, Neuwied, 1962).

Lukács, George, 'Max Weber and German Sociology', *Economy and Society*, Vol. 1, No. 4 (1972).

Malthus, T. R., *An Essay on the Principle of Population* (1798) (Harmondsworth, Penguin, 1970).

Mandelbaum, Maurice, *The Problem of Historical Knowledge* (New York, Harper & Row, 1967).

Marcuse, Herbert, 'Industrialism and Capitalism in the Work of Max Weber', *Negations* (London, Allen Lane, 1968).

Marx, Karl, 'Introduction' to *A Contribution to the Critique of Political Economy* (1857) (London, Lawrence & Wishart, 1971).

Marx, Karl, 'Preface' to the above (1859).

Marx, Karl, *The Civil War in France*, Selected Works, Vol. 1 (1871). (Moscow, F.L.P.H., 1962).

Marx, Karl, *The Critique of the Gotha Programme*, Selected Works, Vol. 2 (1875).

Marx, Karl, *Capital*, Vol. III (1894) (Moscow, F.L.P.H., 1962).

Melman, Seymour, *Decision Making and Productivity* (Oxford, Blackwell, 1956).

Michels, Robert, *Political Parties* (New York, The Free Press, 1962).

Mommsen, Wolfgang, 'Max Weber's Political Sociology and his Philosophy of World History', *International Social Science Journal*, Vol. 17 (1965).

Mommsen, Wolfgang, *The Age of Bureaucracy* (Oxford, Blackwell, 1974).

Morgan, Lewis Henry, *Ancient Society* (1877) (Reprinted Cleveland, Meridian Books, 1963).

Opler, M. E., 'Integration, Evolution and Morgan', *Current Anthropology*, Vol. 3 (1962).

Opler, M. E., 'Reply to Harding and Leacock', *Current Anthropology*, Vol. 5, No. 2 (1964).

Peel, J. D. Y., *Herbert Spencer* (London, Heinemann, 1971).

Rádl, Emanuel, *The History of Biological Theories* (London, O.U.P., 1930).

Rickert, Heinrich, *Science and History* (Princeton, Van Nostrand, 1962).

Sahlins, Marshall and Service, Elman R., *Evolution and Culture* (Ann Arbor, University of Michigan Press, 1960).

Spencer, Herbert, *The Study of Sociology* (London, Kegan Paul, 1880).

Spencer, Herbert, *On Social Evolution* (ed. J. D. Y. Peel) (Chicago, Chicago University Press, 1972).

Terray, Emmanuel, *Marxism and 'Primitive Societies'* (New York, Monthly Review Press, 1972).

Vorzimmer, Peter, *Charles Darwin, the Years of Controversy* (London, University of London Press, 1972).

Weber, Max, *The Methodology of the Social Sciences* (Chicago, Free Press, 1949).

Weber, Max, *The Protestant Ethic and the Spirit of Capitalism* (London, George Allen & Unwin, 1965).

Weber, Max, *Economy and Society* (3 vols) (New York, Bedminster Press, 1969).

Worsley, Peter, 'The Origin of the Family Revisited', *Marxist*, Vol. 4, No. 1 (1965).

Index